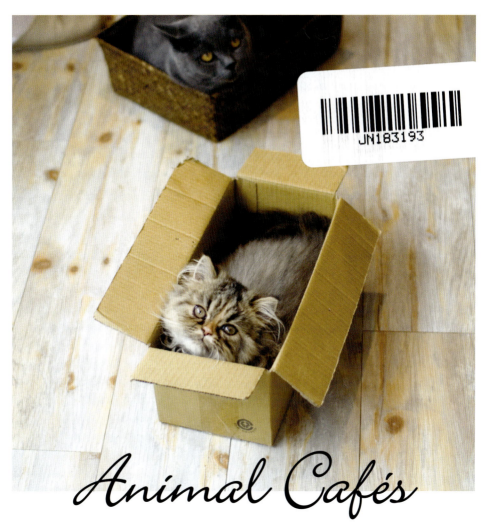

Animal Cafés

This thoroughly researched and lavishly illustrated guide book will introduce you to dozens of the best cafes with the friendliest animals, and offer insider tips on how to have the most fun during your visit.

Robb Satterwhite & Richard Jeffery

Cat Cafés

The atmosphere at a typical cat cafe can vary by time of day — sometimes the resident cats are all napping, sometimes they're running around chasing each other and playing with cat toys. Mornings and weekday evenings tend to be the best time to see active and lively cats.

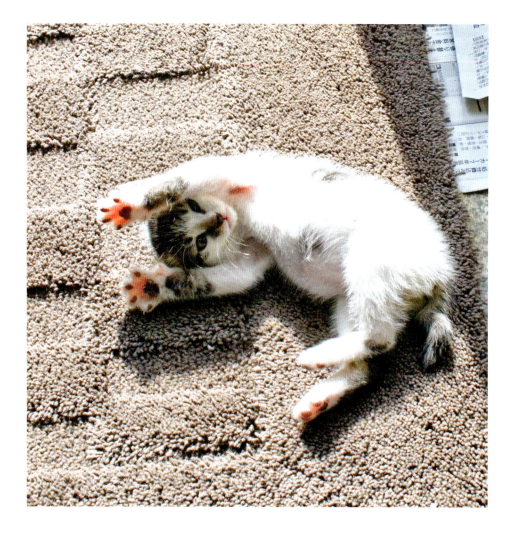

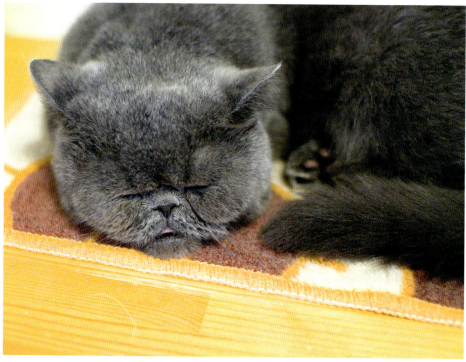

Bird Cafés

Many devotees of owl cafes return week after week to spend time hanging out with their favorite birds – they say it's an excellent way to unwind from the stresses of the workday.
Cafes with parrots and parakeets, on the other hand, provide a very noisy, colorful and fun atmosphere for visitors.

Rabbit Cafés

Animal cafes specializing in rabbits are usually set up like mini pet shops, with most rabbits in cages and just one or two running around loose at any given time. Visitors can also pet and feed the rabbits in their cages, and request a "rabbit exchange" from time to time.

Contents

目 次

1) Introduction to animal cafes・18
   What's an animal cafe?・18
   History of animal cafes・20
2) Visiting an animal cafe・22
   Cat cafes・22
   Bird cafes・22
   Rabbit cafes・24
3) General rules and etiquette・26

Online map of animal cafes・28

1) 動物カフェ入門・19
   動物カフェとは・19
   動物カフェの歴史・21
2) 動物カフェに入ってみよう・23
   猫カフェ・23
   鳥カフェ・23
   うさぎカフェ・25
3) 一般的なルールとエチケット・27

動物カフェのオンラインマップ・28

Cats   ネコ 29
And a few more animals   70

Owls, Hawks   フクロウ・タカ etc. 73
And a few more animals   90

Tropical birds   インコ・オウム etc. 93
And a few more animals   102

Rabbits   うさぎ 105
And a few more animals   122

1) Introduction to animal cafes

What's an animal cafe?

Animal cafes are commercial establishments where you can enjoy the company of resident cats, rabbits, birds or other animals while you lounge around and drink coffee. Cat cafes are the most numerous and well-known type, with a history in Japan going back to 2004, while cafes featuring owls and other birds have been gaining in popularity since around 2014.

Cat cafes are generally set up with one or two playrooms where you can observe and interact with the cats and also drink coffee and tea or have a snack. Many playrooms are furnished like apartment living rooms, but with lots of extra perches, shelves and boxes for the cats to hang out in, while others feel more like kindergarten classrooms, with brightly colored furnishings and toys strewn across the floor. Soft drinks, and sometimes beer and cocktails, are available for human consumption, and many cafes also provide kitty treats for you to dispense.

Rabbit cafes, unlike cat cafes, are usually set up with separate cafe and playroom areas. Generally only a small number of rabbits are allowed to run around at one time, while the others nibble on hay in their cages. Rabbits always seem to be hungry, so feeding them little treats is the most effective way to keep their interest. A few rabbit cafes are nothing more than pet shops that have set up some floor cushions in a corner, while others are more comfortably furnished and equipped.

Large-bird cafes—those featuring owls, hawks and falcons—come in different styles. Some let you hold the birds on your arm like a falconer would do, while others are hands-off—you can take photographs and engage in staring contests, but you're not allowed to touch the birds. Small-bird cafes are less common, and usually these are set up like regular cafes where parakeets and other birds

1) 動物カフェ入門

動物カフェとは

　動物カフェとは店内でコーヒーを飲んでくつろぎながら、猫、うさぎ、鳥などの動物たちとのふれあいが楽しめる商業施設だ。最も数が多く、知名度の高い猫カフェが日本に誕生したのは2004年のこと。2014年あたりから、フクロウや他の鳥類を呼びものにしたカフェが人気を集めるようになっている。

　一般的な猫カフェはプレイルームをひとつか2つ備えていて、じっくり眺めたり、遊んだり、コーヒーやお茶を飲んだり、軽く食事ができるようになっている。プレイルームの多くはマンションのリビングのような室内だが、猫が楽しめるように、猫用の止まり木や、棚や箱がたくさん置いてある。明るい色の家具が置いてあり、床にはおもちゃが散らかっている、まるで幼稚園のような場所もある。ほとんどのカフェでは、猫のおやつも販売している。猫カフェとは異なり、うさぎカフェはカフェとプレイルームとを分けている。たいていは一度に限られた数のうさぎしか自由に歩いておらず、残りはケージの中で干し草をかじっている。うさぎはいつもお腹をすかせているみたいだから、ちょっとしたおやつがあると、こちらに注意を引くのにとても役に立つ。なかには、部屋の片隅に座布団が置いてあるだけで、ペットショップとたいして変わらないうさぎカフェもあるが、居心地よく家具を配置して整えている店がほとんどだ。

　フクロウ、鷹、ハヤブサなど、猛禽類カフェはまた違ったスタイルだ。鷹匠のように腕に鳥を止まらせることができる店もあるが、鳥に触れない店もある。そのような店では、手で触れることはできないが、写真を撮ったり、にらめっこしたりはできる。小鳥カフェはあまり多くない。たいていは普通の喫茶店のような雰囲気だが、コーヒーを飲み、ケーキを食べる背後

provide a colorful and noisy backdrop to your coffee and cake. Other less-common types of animal cafe feature resident dogs, reptiles and other animals.

History of animal cafes

According to some sources, the first cat cafe to open in Japan was Neko no Jikan or Time for Cats in Osaka in March 2004. The boom really took off in 2007, with the help of media attention, and suddenly there were forty cat cafes across the land. Cat cafes became a popular dating venue for young couples, and by 2014, there were nearly 200 feline coffee shops from Kagoshima to Hokkaido. (The boom even spread abroad as cat cafes stretched their claws to Europe, North America and Southeast Asia.)

Pet shops and pet hotels were quick to see the potential, and similar rabbit, bird and dog cafes started to spring up. First came the rabbit cafes, as rabbit shops realized they could make more money renting their bunnies rather than selling them. (As many rabbit shops learned, everyone wants a fluffy baby bunny but nobody wants a 6kg adult thumper.) Since 2014, there's been a boom in owl cafes as stressed city folk flock to tiny rooms full of hooters for some ornithological healing.

There are many reasons for the success of animal cafes in Japan. One main factor is that many people live in apartments where no pets are allowed, or work long hours at jobs that make it impossible for them to keep pets at home. The animal cafe is the perfect answer to their needs: a place to come a few times a month for some healing animal therapy. The fact that many cafes now offer two-hour or three-hour packages shows that there's a market here for some serious, extended pet-bonding time.

で色とりどりのうるさいインコや他の鳥たちが飛び回っている。他に珍しい動物カフェとしては、犬や、は虫類などの動物に会える店がある。

動物カフェの歴史

　複数の資料によると、日本で最初の猫カフェは2004年3月に大阪でオープンした〈猫の時間〉だ。メディアが注目してブームに火がついたのは2007年で、全国で猫カフェが一気に40件オープンした。猫カフェは若いカップルの人気デートスポットとなり、2014年の時点で、北海道から鹿児島まで200店近くもある。(ブームは海を越え、猫カフェ人気はヨーロッパ、北米、東南アジアにまで及んでいる)

　ペットショップやペットホテルがすぐにチャンスに気づいたため、似たようなうさぎ、鳥、犬のカフェが生まれた。一番早かったのはうさぎカフェだ。販売よりもレンタルのほうが利益が出ることに、うさぎを扱う業者が気づいたのだ。(誰もがふわふわの子うさぎを欲しがるが、成長して6キロもある大人のうさぎは見向きもされないことを、業者は分かっていた)2014年からはフクロウカフェのブームが起こり、ストレスを抱えた都市の住人が、フクロウのお姉さんたちが待っている小部屋に鳥類学的癒しを求めて押しかけるようになった。

　日本での動物カフェの成功にはいくつかの理由がある。最大の要因は、多くの日本人がペット禁止の共同住宅に住んでいるか、長時間労働のために、家でペットを飼えないことだ。動物カフェはこういう人々のニーズに完璧に応えている。癒しの動物カフェセラピーを求め、月に数回訪れる場所となっている。最近では2～3時間のコースを提供するカフェがいくつもあって、長い時間をかけた心からのペットとのふれあいが求められているということが分かる。

2) Visiting an animal cafe

Cat cafes

A visitor's experience at a cat cafe can vary quite a bit depending on the time of day and day of the week. Weekday mornings when a cafe first opens are generally the best time to encounter playful, friendly cats, whereas late on weekend evenings you're more likely to encounter cats that are tired and bored with visitors.

Feeding times, which are sometimes listed on a cafe's website, are another good time to arrive. Cats sleep a lot, and it's not unusual to find two-thirds of the residents napping at any given time, but they all wake up for lunch or dinner. Early evenings on weekdays can also be a good time to drop in, as cats are generally more active around sunset. As a general rule, cafes with spacious, comfortable playrooms and a large number of resident cats tend to be the most fun for visitors.

Most cafes follow the same procedure. You'll be asked to leave your shoes in a shoebox at the door and put on some slippers, store your bag in a locker, and wash and sanitize your hands. After selecting your preferred length of stay and possibly a drink, you're free to hang out in the playroom with the cats, play games, read manga, and relax.

Bird cafes

Because of the popularity of bird cafes and the small size of the venues, it's generally recommended that you make a reservation online or by phone. When you arrive, there's usually a short bird-handling lecture in Japanese, often with English-language information on a crib sheet. Most owl cafes now are very interactive, and you'll be told how to slowly approach a bird, gently stroke its head and back, and never ruffle its feathers or

2) 動物カフェに入ってみよう

猫カフェ

　猫カフェでの体験は時間帯や曜日によって違ったものになる。たいていは、開店したばかりの平日の午前中がベストで、元気のいい、人なつこい猫たちに会える。これが週末の夕方ともなると、客に飽きてしまった猫が多いだろう。

　猫の食事の時間が、カフェのホームページに記載されている場合もあるが、この時間に合わせるのもいい。猫はとにかくよく眠るので、どの時間帯でもほとんどの猫がウトウトしているということも珍しくない。しかし、昼食や夕食の時間になれば起きてくる。平日の夕方の早いうちに行ってみるのもいい。猫は通常、日暮れごろが一番活動的だからだ。一般的には、広くて気持ちのよいプレイルームがあって、猫がたくさんいるカフェならば、満足度は高くなるはずだ。

　ほとんどのカフェで同じ手順を踏む。入り口の靴箱に靴を入れ、スリッパに履きかえ、ロッカーに荷物を入れて、手を洗い、消毒するように指示がある。お好みの滞在時間と、場合によっては飲み物を選べば、あとは気ままに猫とプレイルームに居座って、ゲームをしたり、マンガを読んだりしてくつろげる。

鳥カフェ

　鳥カフェは人気があり、店内も広くはないので、通常はネットか電話で予約するのがおすすめ。店に入ると、鳥との接し方について短い説明が日本語である。英語で説明を書いた小さな紙が用意されている場合も多い。現在、多くのフクロウカフェでは鳥にさわることができる。ゆっくりと近づいて、頭や背中をやさしくなでるように、毛を逆立てたり、腹や足をなでると噛んだりつついたりするからやめるように、などの指示があるだろう。鳥を手に乗せるときは、いつも自分から少し離しておくとよい。そうすれ

stroke its belly or feet—which could result in a peck or a bite. When handling a bird, always hold the bird slightly away from you, so that even if it does poop, your clothes and shoes stay clean. If the bird has a lead, make sure to hold onto it tightly until the staff take over.

Flash photography is strictly prohibited in bird cafes because most owls are nocturnal predators and their huge eyes are extremely delicate. Animal lovers can rest assured that all the birds in Japanese bird cafes are bred and raised as pets, as it is illegal to keep wild birds in captivity here. Despite being tame, there's a reason the raptors are kept tethered to their perches: otherwise the larger eagle-owls would eat the tiny pygmy owls for lunch.

Rabbit cafes

The rules for rabbit cafes are similar to cat cafes: change your shoes for slippers, wash and sanitize your hands, and store your bag in a locker or at your table. You can generally choose a rabbit to play with, but ask the staff for advice about rabbit personalities. If you just want to play, then a frisky, jumping bunny is ideal. For photo ops, a more docile and placid rabbit might be more appropriate.

Because rabbits poop a lot, many cafes now issue customers with protective aprons, diapers and paper towels. While poop is easy to avoid, rabbit pee can be surprisingly copious: it's best not to creep up on a bunny from behind as a startled rabbit can shoot a sudden jet of pee about a meter.

ば、フンが落ちても服や靴が汚れずにすむ。もし鳥が紐でつながれていたら、スタッフに引き渡すときまで、しっかり持っているようにしよう。

フクロウの大半は夜行性のハンターなので、大きな目はとてもデリケートだ。フラッシュ付きの写真撮影は鳥カフェでは厳禁。日本では、野生動物の飼育は法律で禁じられている。日本の鳥カフェの鳥たちはペットとして繁殖され、育てられていると聞けば、動物愛護に熱心な人も安心できるだろう。飼育されているとはいえ、猛禽類は止まり木に紐でつないでおかなければならない。大型のワシミミズクが小型のスズメフクロウを食べてしまう危険性があるからだ。

うさぎカフェ

うさぎカフェのルールは猫カフェと似ている。靴をスリッパに履きかえ、手を洗って消毒し、ロッカーか席で持ち物をしまう。たいていどのうさぎと遊びたいか選べるが、スタッフにうさぎの性格を聞いておくとよいだろう。ただ遊びたいだけなら、元気に跳ね回る子が最適だ。写真撮影がご希望なら、比較的おとなしく、落ち着いた子のほうがよいだろう。

うさぎはフンの量が多いので、エプロンや、おむつ、紙タオルを貸してくれる店も多い。フンをよけるのは難しくないが、おしっこは大量だ。びっくりすると、いきなり1メートル近くも飛ばすことがあるので、背後からこっそり近づかないように。

3) General rules and etiquette

Tokyo animal cafes offer differing levels of support for non-Japanese speakers—there's usually (but not always) some sort of instruction sheet in English. Nevertheless the rules tend to be pretty straightforward—be gentle and respectful with the animals, don't bother them when they're asleep or eating, always turn off the flash on your camera, and sanitize your hands at the beginning and end of your visit.

Most venues take no responsibility for any soiling of clothes by animal or bird droppings, accidental scratches or bites, or any previously unknown pet allergies or animal phobias that suddenly become apparent. Most venues are kept scrupulously clean, and staff are on hand to clean up any accidents as soon as they happen.

Long-sleeve shirts or tops are recommended whatever the season, since animal claws and bird talons, or the occasional iguana toenail, can leave scratches.

3) 一般的なルールとエチケット

　東京周辺の動物カフェでは、日本語が分からない人へのサポートがいろいろある。通常は（必ずあるとは限らないが）英語で注意事項を書いた用紙をもらえる。しかし、ルールはいたって簡単だ。動物にはやさしく接し、大切にすること。眠っていたり、食事をしていたらさわらないでおこう。カメラのフラッシュは常にオフにする。入店するときと、帰るときには手を消毒すること。

　動物や鳥のフンで服が汚れたり、思いがけずひっかかれたり、かみつかれたり、ペットアレルギーや動物恐怖症を突然発症しても、たいてい店側は責任をとらない。ほとんどすべての店では、すみずみまで掃除が行き渡っており、汚してしまったときは、控えているスタッフがすぐにきれいにしてくれる。

　季節に関係なく、長袖のシャツやトップスを着ていくのがおすすめだ。動物、鳥の爪や、時にはイグアナの鋭い爪で傷つけられることがあるからだ。

Online map of animal cafes 動物カフェのオンラインマップ

An online map showing the cafes covered in this book can be found at http://animalcafes.com/acmap.html or http://bit.ly/ac-map

本書で紹介している動物カフェが探せるオンラインマップはこちら：
http://animalcafes.com/acmap.html
または http://bit.ly/ac-map

Note: cover charge information refers to basic cover charges – other, extended plans may also be available. All information listed here is subject to change.
注意　サービス料は基本料金のみの表示となっている。さらにオプションが追加できる場合もある。ここに記載するすべての情報は変更となる場合がある。

装幀：アキヨシアキラ
本文デザイン・DTP：ギルド

※掲載の内容は 2015 年 8 月現在のものです。

ネコ

Cats

Nekoya
Omiya

While the cats and kittens here are well taken care of by the solicitous staff, Nekoya also goes out of its way to make human visitors welcome, with comfortable massage chairs, a big library of manga to read, and free WiFi. There's plenty of room for both people and cats to stretch out in the spacious playroom—the largest in the Tokyo area.

We happened to arrive during snack time (around 6pm), and we were given a handful of cat treats to dole out as we saw fit, which helped us make friends quickly, if perhaps only briefly. The staff stay busy keeping the seventeen cats here entertained with various toys, and the residents include several playful kittens, which keeps things lively.

The cat breeds here include all your favorite cute and photogenic breeds such as Scottish Fold, Himalayan, Bengal, Norwegian Forest, Munchkin and Exotic Shorthair, and some more exotic types including a Japanese Bobtail, Devon Rex and a cross between a Russian Blue and an American Curl.

Pricing plans start from one hour, and drinks are 100 yen each—just help yourself from the well-stocked refrigerator.

Overall: ☕☕☕☕☕☕☕
総合評価

Visitor amenities: ☕☕☕☕☕
店内設備

Animal interactivity: ☕☕☕☕☕
動物とのふれあい

猫屋

大宮

〈猫屋〉ではよく気がつくスタッフによる猫たちのケアが行き届いているのみならず、快適なマッサージチェアや大量のマンガや、無料Wi-Fiがあって、人間の客へのもてなしも十分だ。関東圏最大の広々としたプレイルームでは、人も猫も体を伸ばすことができる。

入店したときはたまたま軽食タイムで（午後6時ごろ）猫用おやつをひとにぎりもらってあげることができた。ちょっとの間だけだが、猫とすぐに仲良くなれるので、これはいいと思った。スタッフがしきりにいろいろなおもちゃで猫を楽しませていた。元気な子猫が何匹かいたので、とてもにぎやかだった。

かわいらしい、写真映えする品種の猫たちがそろっている。スコティッシュフォールド、ヒマラヤン、ベンガル、ノルウェージャンフォレストキャット、マンチカン、エキゾチックショートヘアなどだ。さらに、もっと珍しいジャパニーズボブテイルや、デボンレックス、ロシアンブルーとアメリカンカールの交配種もいる。

料金プランは1時間からで、飲み物は100円。品揃え豊富な冷蔵庫から自由にとることができる。

🕐 Data Box

Resident animals 店内にいる動物	cats	猫
Station 最寄駅	Omiya	大宮
Cover charge 基本料金	1,000 yen for one hour, 200 yen for each additional 15 minutes	1時間 1,000円　延長は15分ごとに 200円
Open hours 営業時間	11am-10pm (last admission 9pm)	11:00〜22:00（最終入場は21:00）
Address 住所	Saitama-shi, Omiya-ku, Daimoncho 2-11, Prosper one Bldg. 5F [5 minutes from Omiya station East Exit (JR and Tobu lines)]	さいたま市大宮区大門町2-11 プロスパーワンビル5F [大宮駅（JR線、東武鉄道）から徒歩5分]
Cafe menu カフェメニュー	soft drinks 100 yen	各種ソフトドリンク 100円
Animal treats 動物のおやつ	cat snacks	猫用スナック

Website: http://www.nekoyacafe.com/oomiya/

Phone: 048-644-0660

Miysis
Yokohama Kannai

Somehow the residents at Miysis seem friendlier and more playful than the usual cat cafe denizens. Perhaps they're just happier in their environment—the playroom here is a big, sprawling space designed to keep cats content, with lots of carpeted trees to climb and upholstery to shred, as well as numerous spots in which to perch or nap.

Visitor amenities here are also above average. The sofas are reasonably comfortable, if you don't mind the fact that they double as scratching posts, and the background music is an invigorating mix of soul and R&B. There are shelves full of Japanese manga and magazines, many of them cat-themed, to peruse.

Even the iced coffee—served with real milk—is quite drinkable. Other beverage options include sesame-soy milkshakes and mixed-berry yogurt smoothies, while the snack menu offers sweets and Chinese-style rice balls.

If you're interested in pedigrees, the twenty resident cats include a couple of Scottish Folds, a short-legged Munchkin and a very fluffy Siberian, along with some less exotic breeds. An English-language orientation sheet is provided for visitors, and binders introducing the cats are available for inspection.

Overall: ☕☕☕☕☕☕☕
総合評価

Visitor amenities: ☕☕☕☕
店内設備

Animal interactivity: ☕☕☕☕☕
動物とのふれあい

キャットカフェ　ミーシス　　横浜市関内

　〈ミーシス〉の猫たちは普通の猫カフェよりも元気で人なつこい気がする。きっと、住んでいる場所に満足しているのだろう。プレイルームは大きく広々として、猫を満足させるものだし、自由に登れる布張りのキャットタワーや、爪でビリビリにしてもいいクッション材がたくさん置いてある。飛び乗ったり、眠ったりする場所もあちこちにある。

　店内の設備も平均以上だ。爪とぎのあとが気にならなければ、ソファはまあまあ快適だし、BGMはソウルとR&Bをとりまぜた軽快なものだ。棚には日本のマンガや雑誌が並んでいて、猫関係のものも多く、じっくり読むことができる。

　本物のミルクと一緒に出てくるアイスコーヒーもおいしい。飲み物は他に黒ゴマと豆乳のシェイクやミックスベリーのヨーグルトスムージーなどがあり、食べ物はスイーツや中華ちまきがある。

　血統について書いておくと、20匹の猫たちの中にはスコティッシュフォールドや短足のマンチカン、ふわふわのシベリア猫たちがそれぞれ2、3匹いて、他にはよく見かける品種もいる。英語での注意事項を書いた用紙をもらえる。猫を紹介したバインダーも閲覧可能。

🕐 Data Box

Resident animals 店内にいる動物	cats	猫
Station 最寄駅	Kannai	関内駅
Cover charge 基本料金	1,300 yen for 70 minutes with one drink	70分ワンドリンク付きで1,300円
Open hours 営業時間	Noon-8pm; 11am-8pm on weekends (last admission 7pm)	12:00～20:00、土日は11:00～20:00（最終入店は19:00）
Address 住所	Yokohama-shi, Naka-ku, Chojamachi 6-99 [5 minutes from Kannai station (JR line)]	横浜市中区長者町6-99　[JR関内駅から徒歩5分]
Cafe menu カフェメニュー	soft drinks from 300 yen, snacks from 350 yen	ソフトドリンク300円から、軽食350円から
Animal treats 動物のおやつ	none	なし

Website: http://www.cat-miysis.com/　　　　Phone: 045-325-7166

Temari no Ouchi
Kichijoji

Typical of Tokyo's second wave of cat cafes, Temari no Ouchi strives to create a destination "relaxation space" rather than just a place to play with cats for thirty minutes. It bills itself as a "forest of wondrous cats" and the fairytale decor makes you think you're attending a Mad Hatter's tea party in a gingerbread house.

Kick back with an imported beer or original cocktail, or choose from a range of herbal teas and coffee-based drinks. There's also an extensive menu of desserts, light snacks (popcorn shrimp, sausages), and full meals (keema curry, Hawaiian loco moco).

The spacious, cartoonish main playroom provides ample seating for dozens of visitors, and incorporates numerous perches, nooks and crannies for the seventeen resident cats to prowl. There are some rare breeds here including Chartreux, Scottish Fold, Norwegian Forest Cat, Bombay and Persian Chinchilla, as well as the more familiar American Shorthair, Munchkin, Ragamuffin and Ragdolls.

Weekday evenings are a good time to visit, as there's a flurry of feline activity when feeding time starts at six-thirty. Free WiFi is available.

Overall: ☕☕☕☕☕☕☕
総合評価

Visitor amenities: ☕☕☕☕☕
店内設備

Animal interactivity: ☕☕☕☕
動物とのふれあい

てまりのおうち

吉祥寺

都内の後発の猫カフェによくあるのだが、〈てまりのおうち〉では、30分猫とただ遊ぶだけではない、「くつろぎの場所」を提供しようとしているようだ。店によると、ここは「不思議な猫の森」で、おとぎの国のように飾りつけてある店内に入れば、ジンジャーブレッド・ハウスでアリスのお茶会に出席している気分になる。

輸入ビールやオリジナルのカクテル、もしくはハーブティーやコーヒー系の飲み物を選んでくつろごう。他にもメニューはあり、デザートや軽食(ポップコーンシュリンプやソーセージ)、しっかりした食事(キーマカレーやロコモコ)が注文できる。

広々としたおとぎの国のようなメインプレイルームには人間が座る場所がたくさんあって、いたるところに設置してあるキャットタワーや、隠れ場所や、すき間を猫たちが行ったり来たりしている。シャルトリュー、スコティッシュフォールド、ノルウェージャンフォレストキャット、ボンベイ、チンチラなどの珍しい猫がいる。他にも、アメリカンショートヘア、マンチカン、ラガマフィン、ラグドールがいる。

平日の夕方がねらい目だ。6時半の食事どきには猫の動きが活発になる。無料Wi-Fi利用可。

Data Box

Resident animals 店内にいる動物	cats	猫
Station 最寄駅	Kichijoji	吉祥寺
Cover charge 基本料金	1,200 yen; 1,600 yen on weekends and holidays; 700 yen after 7pm	1,200円 土日祝日は1,600円 19時以降は700円
Open hours 営業時間	10am-9pm, last admission 8:30pm	10:00～21:00 最終入場は20:30
Address 住所	Musashino-shi, Kichijoji Honcho 2-13-14 Musashi Forum III 3F [5 minutes from Kichijoji station (JR and Inokashira lines)]	東京都武蔵野市吉祥寺本町2-13-14 武蔵フォーラムIII 3階 [吉祥寺駅(JR線、井の頭線)から徒歩5分]
Cafe menu カフェメニュー	coffee, tea and soft drinks from 400 yen, beer from 530 yen, cakes from 480 yen, meals from 780 yen	コーヒー、お茶、ソフトドリンク400円から ビール530円から ケーキ480円から 食事780円から
Animal treats 動物のおやつ	none	なし

Website: http://www.temarinoouchi.com/   Phone: 0422-23-5503

Miacis
Kobe Motomachi

A nice contrast to the sleepy atmosphere of your typical cat cafe, Miacis was positively frenetic with activity during our evening visit, with cats running amok and chasing one another across the length of the spacious playroom. When we entered we were asked to tread carefully as there might be kittens underfoot, and indeed we counted at least five kittens among the resident population of twenty, all of them quite frisky.

One of the most popular furnishings is a nylon-clad Y-shaped tunnel structure which cats enjoy alternately crawling through and pouncing on after running the length of the room. Perhaps because of all this vigorous activity, the cats here seem friendlier and more outgoing than average, some of them spontaneously approaching visitors rather than waiting passively.

Open since early 2015, Miacis is large and comfortably furnished, set up like a huge living room. The shop is up on the second floor, with floor-to-ceiling windows offering a nice view out over Motomachi's main shopping arcade.

Vintage jazz plays on the soundtrack, and the rules here are more relaxed than usual—for example you can pick up the cats and hold them if you do so gently. Coffee and other drinks are available but optional.

Overall: ☕☕☕☕☕☕
総合評価

Visitor amenities: ☕☕☕
店内設備

Animal interactivity: ☕☕☕
動物とのふれあい

Cat Cafe Miacis ねこまみれ　神戸 元町

　よくある眠たい雰囲気の猫カフェとは違い、夕方〈ミアキス〉に入ると大騒ぎの最中で、猫たちが広々としたプレイルームじゅうをドタバタ走り回って、追いかけっこしていた。子猫を踏まないように足元には気をつけるように言われたのだが、元気な20匹の猫のなかには、少なくとも5匹の子猫がいた。
　ナイロン生地で覆われた、Y字型のキャットトンネルが大人気で、部屋じゅうを走り回った猫たちが、次から次へとやってきては中にもぐりこんだり、飛び乗ったりしていた。このように元気に遊んでいるので、ここの猫たちは他よりも人なつこくて、積極的なのだろう。受け身で待つのではなく、自分から近づいてくる猫もいるくらいだ。
　2015年3月にオープンした〈ミアキス〉の店内は広く、くつろげる家具も置いてあり、まるで大きなリビングルームのようだ。店は2階にあって、床から天井まである窓からは元町の商店街の様子を眺めることができる。
　ビンテージジャズが流れる店内のルールは、そんなに厳しいものではない。例えば、やさしく扱うのであれば、自分で猫を選んでだっこすることができる。コーヒーなどの飲み物があるが、別料金となっている。

Data Box

Resident animals 店内にいる動物	cats	猫
Station 最寄駅	Kobe Motomachi	元町
Cover charge 基本料金	1,000 yen for one hour; 1,200 on weekends and holidays	1時間 1,000円　土日祝日は 1,200円
Open hours 営業時間	10am-9pm, last admission 8pm. Closed Mondays, Tuesdays	10:00〜21:00 最終入場 20:00 月曜、火曜定休
Address 住所	Kobe-shi, Chuo-ku, Motomachi-dori 5-4-8, Sanki Bldg 202 [2 minutes from Kobe Motomachi station (JR Tokaido line)]	神戸市中央区元町通 5-4-8 三木ビル202 [元町駅JR東海道線、阪神線) から徒歩 2 分]
Cafe menu カフェメニュー	soft drinks 300 yen	各種ソフトドリンク 300円
Animal treats 動物のおやつ	none	なし

Website: http://www2.hp-ez.com/hp/miacis-m　　　Phone: 080-4242-6924

Nyankoto
Takadanobaba

Nyankoto has some of the prettiest cats in town—all thirteen of the residents have impressive pedigrees, and the two frisky Exotic Shorthair kittens are especially cute. The little booklet introducing the cats by name also lists an unusual Kinkalow (a cross between a Munchkin and an American Curl) and Lambkin (Selkirk Rex and Munchkin cross), along with three Munchkins, a Selkirk Rex, a Ragamuffin, a Himalayan and an American Curl, among others. In comparison, the lone Persian in the house seems as commonplace as an alleycat.

The cats here are also among the liveliest we've encountered—one extra-friendly fellow actually managed to jump on our shoulder while we were putting our bag in a locker. The pen we were using to take notes with provided endless amusement whenever it was knocked to the floor, and the mirrored base of our table served as another popular source of entertainment.

The playroom is relatively large by cat-cafe standards, with a couple of benches up front and a table you can sit at if you don't want to stretch out on the floor. Drinks are free—just help yourself from the vending machine—but be careful where you put them down. Cat treats are 100 yen.

Overall: 🍵🍵🍵🍵🍵🍵🍵
総合評価

Visitor amenities: 🍵🍵🍵🍵
店内設備

Animal interactivity: 🍵🍵🍵🍵
動物とのふれあい

にゃんこと

高田馬場

〈にゃんこと〉の猫たちは、このエリアで一、二を争うほどのかわいさだ。店内の猫たち13匹はすべてしっかりした血統を持っている。なかでも、よく動くエキゾチックショートヘアの子猫2匹は抜群にかわいい。猫の名前を紹介した小冊子には珍しいキンカロー（マンチカンとアメリカンカールとの交配種）やラムキン（セルカークレックスとマンチカンとの交配種）、他にもマンチカン3匹とセルカークレックス、ラガマフィン、ヒマラヤン、アメリカンカールが1匹ずつと、その他の猫がのっている。珍しい猫たちと比べると、店内で唯一のペルシャ猫がそのあたりの猫と同じようにありふれたものに思えてしまう。

取材したなかでは、ここの猫たちが一番積極的だった。私たちがロッカーに荷物を入れていると、並外れて人なつっこい猫が一匹肩に乗ってきたぐらいだ。メモをとるためのペンが床にころがればいつまでもじゃれているし、テーブルベースが鏡面になっていて、楽しく遊んでいた。

他の猫カフェに比べ、プレイルームは広い。入ったところにいくつかベンチがあるし、床にいるのに飽きたら座っていられるテーブル席もある。飲み物は無料。自動のベンダーから自由に用意することができる。飲み物を置く場所には気をつけよう。猫のおやつは100円だ。

🕐 Data Box

Resident animals 店内にいる動物	cats	猫
Station 最寄駅	Takadanobaba	高田馬場
Cover charge 基本料金	800 yen for one hour, 200 yen for each additional 15 minutes	1時間 800円　延長は15分ごとに 200円
Open hours 営業時間	Open hours: 11am-10pm	11:00 ～ 22:00
Address 住所	Shinjuku-ku, Takadanobaba 2-14-6, Swan Bldg 201 [2 minutes from Takadanobaba station (JR, Seibu and Tozai lines)]	東京都新宿区高田馬場 2-14-6 スワンビル 201 [高田馬場駅（JR線、西武鉄道、東西線）から徒歩 2 分]
Cafe menu カフェメニュー	unlimited soft drinks	各種ソフトドリンクが豊富
Animal treats 動物のおやつ	cat snacks 100 yen	猫ケーキ 100円

Website: http://www.nyankoto.com　　　　Phone: 03-6233-9662

Calico
Shinjuku Kabukicho

Even when it's full of visitors, there are plenty of cats to go around at this spacious, long-established two-story cafe. The shop's website promises more than fifty different cats, and that seems about right—while we were there we noticed a few new cats arriving in carrier boxes, perhaps being brought in to handle the mid-afternoon rush. You'll find many exotic breeds here including the Ocicat, Birman, Chartreux, Singapura, Himalayan and LaPerm, as well as your plain-old, common-or-garden Shorthairs and Munchkins.

The sixth-floor entry area is mostly devoted to lockers and a glassed-in breakroom for off-duty cats, while the main playroom and cafe area is down on the fifth floor. The cafe is full of comfortable sofas as well as a bit of floor seating, and the cafe tables have built-in receptacles to keep drinks from being knocked over. Windows at the front of the room look out onto the busy streets of Shinjuku.

In addition to numerous coffee and tea variations, the cafe serves an inexpensive food menu in a separate glassed-in dining area adjoining the main playroom. Cat snacks—containers of appetizing-looking boiled chicken—are 300 yen, and a very popular option.

Given its convenient location in the heart of Shinjuku, Calico is popular with foreign as well as Japanese customers, and the staff are fluent in English.

Overall: ☕☕☕☕☕☕
総合評価

Visitor amenities: ☕☕☕
店内設備

Animal interactivity: ☕☕☕☕
動物とのふれあい

きゃりこ

新宿歌舞伎町

古くからあり、広々とした店舗が2階にまたがるこちらの店では、客がたくさん入っても多くの猫がうろついている。店のホームページには常に50匹以上の猫がいるとあり、これは本当のようだ。私たちの滞在中も何匹かキャリアボックスに入った新しい猫たちが到着していたが、午後の忙しい時間に対応するためだろう。珍しい品種をたくさんそろえている。オシキャット、バーマン、シャルトリュー、ヒマラヤン、ラパーマの他に、おなじみのショートヘアやマンチカンもいる。

受付のある6階はロッカーと、ガラス張りの猫たちの休憩室がある。メインプレイルームとカフェエリアは5階にある。カフェには座り心地のよいソファが並べてあり、床に座れる席も少しある。カフェテーブルには転倒防止のためにカップホルターがそなえつけてある。正面の窓からは人通りの多い新宿の街を見下ろせる。

メインプレイルームに隣接したガラス張りのカフェコーナーでは豊富なコーヒーやお茶のメニューの他にもリーズナブルな値段のフードメニューがある。人気のある猫のおやつは、容器に入った鶏のささみで、300円だ。

交通アクセスのよい新宿にある〈きゃりこ〉は日本人だけでなく、外国人にも人気だ。店のスタッフは英語がしゃべれる。

🕰 Data Box

Resident animals 店内にいる動物	cats	猫
Station 最寄駅	Shinjuku	新宿
Cover charge 基本料金	1,000 yen for the first hour weekdays, 1,200 yen on weekends	最初の1時間平日は1,000円、土日は1,200円
Open hours 営業時間	10am-10pm daily (LO 9:15pm)	10:00～22:00 (ラストオーダー21:15) 年中無休
Address 住所	Shinjuku-ku, Kabukicho 1-16-2, Fuji Bldg 6F [5 minutes from Shinjuku Station South Exit (JR line)]	新宿区歌舞伎町1-16-2 富士ビルディング6F［新宿駅（JR線、京王線、地下鉄など）南口から徒歩5分］
Cafe menu カフェメニュー	Hot and cold soft drinks from 200 yen, cakes 300 yen and pasta dishes 500 yen	ソフトドリンク（温・冷）200円から ケーキ300円 パスタ500円
Animal treats 動物のおやつ	cat snacks 300 yen	猫のおやつ300円

Website: http://catcafe.jp/shop_shinjyuku.html   Phone: 03-6457-6387

Calico
Kichijoji

The best thing about Calico, one of Tokyo's very first cat cafes, is that there are plenty of cats to go around—some 24 at last count. Perhaps because of the high cat-to-human ratio, the cats here seem more relaxed and more pettable than average. There's a nice mix of exotic (such as the Egyptian Mau and Abyssinian) and more common breeds, most of them very photogenic.

Our most recent visit happened to coincide with feeding time (around 5:30pm). There was quite a build-up of tension in the air while the staff made elaborate preparations as some of the cats were on a special diet and needed to be moved to a different room.

Drinks here are priced at 200 yen and are optional, while cat snacks are available for 300 yen. The snacks are strips of boiled chicken breast, and they proved to be popular with the cats even directly after their regular dinnertime.

Overall: ☕☕☕☕☕☕
総合評価

Visitor amenities: ☕☕☕
店内設備

Animal interactivity: ☕☕☕☕☕
動物とのふれあい

きゃりこ

吉祥寺

東京の猫カフェのなかでも初期にオープンした〈きゃりこ〉のよいところは、店内にたくさん猫がいることだ。数えただけでも24匹はいた。人間に対して猫の割合が高いので、猫たちは比較的のびのびしていて、さわらせてくれる。エジプシャンマウやアビシニアンなどの珍しい品種から一般的な品種までバランスよくそろえている。写真うつりもバッチリだ。

前回訪れたときは偶然食事タイム（午後5時半ごろ）と重なった。スタッフが念入りに作業をしていて、ピリピリしていた。特別な食事をする猫を別室に移動させていたのだ。

飲み物は200円で別に注文できる。猫のおやつが300円で買える。おやつは鶏ささみを細かくしたもので、ごはんを食べたばかりなのに、猫たちに大人気だった。

Data Box

Resident animals 店内にいる動物	cats	猫
Station 最寄駅	Kichijoji	吉祥寺
Cover charge 基本料金	1,000 yen for the first hour weekdays, 1,200 yen on weekends	最初の1時間平日は1,000円、土日は1,200円
Open hours 営業時間	10am-10pm daily (LO 9:15pm)	10:00～22:00（ラストオーダー21:15）年中無休
Address 住所	Musashino-shi, Kichijoji Minamicho 1-5-7, Yuki Bldg 4F [2 minutes from Kichijoji station Park Exit (JR and Inokashira lines)]	武蔵野市吉祥寺南町1-5-7 雪ビル4F［吉祥寺駅（JR線・井の頭線）公園口から徒歩2分］
Cafe menu カフェメニュー	hot and cold soft drinks from 200 yen	ソフトドリンク（温・冷）200円から
Animal treats 動物のおやつ	cat snacks 300 yen	猫のおやつ300円

Website: http://catcafe.jp/shop_kichijyouji.html　　Phone: 0422-29-8353

Nyantsume
Osaka Dotonbori

The scrapbook introducing Nyantsume's twenty resident cats is unusually detailed—not only do you learn each cat's breed and birthday, but English-language descriptions like "sensitive," "innocent," "robust" and "narcissist" give you some insight into their personalities as well. We certainly encountered quite a few lively mousers during a weekday morning visit, with lots of running, chasing and play-fighting among the floor crew.

The playroom is a big L-shaped living room, and cover charge includes a soft drink (beer and cocktails run a bit extra) plus a complimentary container of kitty treats. We've noticed that this policy of cat snacks for all visitors seems to increase the general alertness of the cat population, but further studies are needed.

The residents here are a diverse mix of attractive breeds, including Selkirk Rex, Scottish Fold, Maine Coon, Munchkin and Ragdoll. Two rather outgoing Bengals seemed to be among the ringleaders out on the floor.

Nyantsume (the name roughly means "cat claw marks") is up two flights of stairs in an office building, conveniently located near the eastern end of the main shopping and restaurant street of Dotonbori. The cafe is notable for its early opening hours, from 10am.

Overall: ☕☕☕☕☕☕
総合評価

Visitor amenities: ☕☕☕
店内設備

Animal interactivity: ☕☕☕☕
動物とのふれあい

にゃんつめ

大阪　道頓堀

〈にゃんつめ〉には店の猫たちの非常に詳細な情報を載せたスクラップブックがある。品種や誕生日の情報にとどまらず、それぞれの性格についても英語で「sensitive」（神経質）「innocent」（無邪気）「robust」（エネルギッシュ）「narcissist」（ナルシスト）などと書いてあるのでよく分かる。午前中に訪れたところ、情報通りの元気な猫たちがたくさんいて、仲間同士で走ったり、追いかけっこをしたり、じゃれたりしていた。

プレイルームは、L字型のリビングルームで、基本料金にはソフトドリンクが含まれている（ビールやカクテルは少し高い）。猫のおやつも無料だ。訪れる客が全員猫のおやつを持っていると、猫たちが全体的に注意を向けてくれる効果がある気がする。もっと観察が必要だが。

さまざまな、面白い品種の猫たちをそろえている。セルカークレックス、スコティッシュフォールド、メインクーン、マンチカン、ラグドールなどがいる。とても積極的なベンガルが2匹いて、どうやらボス的存在らしい。

〈にゃんつめ〉（「猫の爪痕」くらいの意味）はオフィスビルの3階にあって、道頓堀の商店やレストランが集まっているメインエリアの東端という便利な場所にある。カフェの開店時間は午前10時と早い。

Data Box

Resident animals 店内にいる動物	cats	猫
Station 最寄駅	Dotonbori	道頓堀
Cover charge 基本料金	1,000 yen for one hour	1時間 1,000 円
Open hours 営業時間	10am-8pm (last admission 7pm). Closed Mondays	10:00 ～ 20:00（最終入場 19:00）月曜定休
Address 住所	Osaka-shi, Chuo-ku, Dotonbori 1-1-7, 3F [2 minutes from Nipponbashi station (Sakaisuji and Sennichimae lines)]	大阪市中央区道頓堀 1-1-7 真幸ビル 3F ［日本橋駅（堺筋線、千日前線）から徒歩2分］
Cafe menu カフェメニュー	soft drinks and alcoholic beverages	各種ソフトドリンク、アルコール飲料
Animal treats 動物のおやつ	free cat treats	猫のおやつ（無料）

Website: http://doraneko.itigo.jp/　　Phone: 06-6213-6100

Melange
Ebisu

Whoever was responsible for the interior design for Nyafe Melange has clearly discovered the secret to a successful cat cafe—providing lots and lots of different places to sit, perch, and nap. At first glance it looks like an ordinary living room, with bookcases, sofas and coffee tables, but there are also dozens of custom-made shelves and tiny stools upon which the 22 resident cats can comfortably sit and preside over cafe business.

The human staff are friendly and attentive—when we took a break to jot down some notes, a staff member brought over a sleepy cat in a basket to keep us company.

Prices are quite reasonable and you don't need to order a beverage, although you can get coffee or tea if you like. WiFi is free.

Overall: ☕☕☕☕☕
総合評価

Visitor amenities: ☕☕☕
店内設備

Animal interactivity: ☕☕☕
動物とのふれあい

ニャフェ　メランジェ　　恵比寿

　〈ニャフェ　メランジェ〉のインテリアは猫カフェ成功のツボを押さえたものとなっている。猫が座ったり、上ったり、眠ったりする場所が数えきれないほど用意してあるのだ。本棚やソファ、コーヒーテーブルが置いてあり、一見普通のリビングみたいだが、オーダーメイドの棚や小さな椅子がいたるところにある。思い思いに腰を下ろした店の22匹の猫たちは、まるでカフェ業務を監督しているようだ。

　人間のスタッフは気さくで親切だ。メモをとろうと休憩していたら、眠っている猫が入ったかごを持ってきて、そばに置いてくれた。

　料金はリーズナブルで、飲み物は注文しなくてもよい。必要なら、コーヒーかお茶を注文できる。無料のWi-Fi接続がある。

🕐 Data Box

Resident animals 店内にいる動物	cats	猫
Station 最寄駅	Ebisu	恵比寿
Cover charge 基本料金	600 yen for 30 minutes, 1,000 yen for one hour (700/1,200 yen on weekends and holidays)	30分 600円　1時間 1,000円（土日祝日はそれぞれ 700円、1,200円）
Open hours 営業時間	Open hours: Noon-8pm daily; Noon-9pm Friday/Saturday	12:00～20:00　金曜、土曜は 12:00～21:00
Address 住所	Shibuya-ku, Ebisu 1-7-13 3F [3 minutes from Ebisu station (JR and Hibiya lines)]	東京都渋谷区恵比寿1-7-13 麻仁ビル恵比寿3F［恵比寿駅から徒歩3分 (JR線、日比谷線)］
Cafe menu カフェメニュー	coffee, tea, and soft drinks 100 yen	コーヒー、お茶、ソフトドリンク 100円
Animal treats 動物のおやつ	cat snacks 100 yen	猫用スナック 100円

Website: http://www.nyafe-melange.com　　Phone: 03-5449-4024

Wan Nyan Chu 2
Kyoto Kawaramachi

This second branch of Kyoto's most popular cat cafe has a quieter, more relaxed atmosphere than the main shop, with plenty of comfortable nooks and crannies for human visitors as well as the twenty resident cats to stretch out in.

The admission price is a bit higher than average, but it's not all that steep considering the cafe's very central location, and you do get a nice cup of green tea and a bean-paste dessert along with your hour of cat time. Cat treats are available for a small additional charge and we recommend them as an efficient way to earn the affection of the sleepy cats here.

The cafe also operates a separate kitten room, and this is the first time we've seen a kitten surcharge—an extra 300 yen for fifteen minutes with the three resident kittens. In other cafes kittens are arbitrarily placed in cages for rest time when they get tired out, so perhaps this arrangement makes sense.

In addition to your complimentary tea and sweets you can order juice or beer a la carte. The shop is located on a side street, up on the third floor of an office building. It shares the floor with a tattoo studio called Catclaw, so be careful not to go to the wrong shop by accident.

Overall: 🍵🍵🍵🍵🍵
総合評価

Visitor amenities: 🍵🍵🍵🍵
店内設備

Animal interactivity: 🍵🍵🍵
動物とのふれあい

犬猫人2 (wan nyan chu two) 京都 河原町

京都で一番人気の猫カフェの2号店であるこの店は、本店よりも静かで落ち着いた雰囲気だ。静かなスペースや、ちょっとした隠れ場がたくさんあって、猫のみならず人間もくつろげる。

入店料は若干高めだが、便利な立地を考えると決して法外な値段ではない。それに、猫と過ごす間、おいしい緑茶とあんこの乗ったデザートを出してくれる。少しの追加料金で猫のおやつを買うことができるが、眠たげな猫たちの心をつかむことができるのでおすすめだ。

別にある子猫部屋に追加料金を払うというシステムははじめてだった。15分300円で3匹の子猫たちと過ごすことができる。他のカフェでは、子猫たちが疲れてしまって、休憩のためにケージに入れられているのを見かけるので、これはよい方法だと思った。

無料のお茶とスイーツの他にも、メニューからジュースやビールを注文できる。大通りから一本入った通りに面したオフィスビルの3階にある。同じ階にはタトゥースタジオの「キャットクロー (Catclaw)」があるから、間違えないように気をつけよう。

🕐 Data Box

Resident animals 店内にいる動物	cats	猫
Station 最寄駅	Kawaramachi	河原町
Cover charge 基本料金	1,500 yen for one hour with tea and sweets	1時間1,500円　お茶、お菓子付き
Open hours 営業時間	Noon-9pm	12:00〜21:00
Address 住所	Kyoto-shi, Nakagyo-ku Iseyacho 354-1, Kyara Bldg. 3F East [5 minutes from Kawaramachi station (Hankyu Kyoto line)]	京都市中京区伊勢谷町354-1 伽羅ビル3F 東　[河原町駅（阪急京都線）から徒歩5分]
Cafe menu カフェメニュー	free tea, juice 150 yen, beer 400 yen	お茶は無料　ジュース150円　ビール400円
Animal treats 動物のおやつ	cat snacks 200 yen	猫用おやつ200円

Website: http://balu.jp/list2.html　　　　**Phone:** 075-746-6858

Marumaru
Oimachi

With its dim lighting, soft music and backdrop of white noise from the ventilation system, Marumaru has a rather languid air, reinforced by the sight of napping cats sprawled everywhere. The cafe is quite spacious, and spread out over one and half floors of a five-story internet cafe that's long and narrow in plan. The upper floor has a computer that you can use, plus the usual collections of books, magazines and comics.

Down on the lower level are lockers and a self-service drinks machine that dispenses free coffee, tea and sodas. We were warned to be sure to attach a lid tightly to our drinks, as apparently drink-toppling is a popular sport here. Also exercise caution on the stairway between the levels, so you don't inadvertently step on any sleeping cats.

Cat snacks are available during certain hours of the day (for 150 yen), and the place really perked up when one of our fellow visitors took the plunge, and encouraged the suddenly alert residents to beg for snacks. Even without bribes though, with 21 cats here there are usually at least a few that are awake and ready to play or be petted. The feline talent includes exotic breeds such as the Somali, Himalayan, Abyssinian, Bengal, Russian Blue and Persian.

Weekday evenings don't seem to be particularly crowded, although weekends of course are a different matter. Young children are welcome, and Thursday is "Men's Day," when male customers get a 200-yen discount.

Overall: ☕☕☕☕☕
総合評価

Visitor amenities: ☕☕☕☕
店内設備

Animal interactivity: ☕☕☕
動物とのふれあい

キャットカフェ　まるまる

大井町

照明が薄暗く、静かな音楽が流れ、換気扇の回る音がブーンと聞こえてくる、物憂げな雰囲気の店だ。あちこちに寝そべっている猫たちもそんな雰囲気作りに一役買っている。店の面積は広く、ウナギの寝床のような5階立てのインターネットカフェの1.5階分を占めている。上階には自由に使えるコンピューターがあり、本、雑誌、マンガもそろっている。下の階にはセルフサービスの飲み物のドリンクサーバーがあって、無料でコーヒー、お茶、炭酸飲料が飲める。猫たちの間で飲み物を倒すゲームがはやっているので、カップのふたはしっかり閉めるよう注意された。フロア間の階段にも気をつけよう。うっかり寝ている猫を踏んでしまうかもしれない。

猫のおやつは日中の決まった時間に買える(150円)。一緒に行った仲間がおやつを買ってみたのだが、猫たちが突然そわそわしだして、群がってきた。おやつのような貢ぎ物がなくても、ここには21匹も猫がいるのでいつも2、3匹は起きていて遊んだりなでたりできる。ソマリ、ヒマラヤン、アビシニアン、ベンガル、ロシアンブルー、ペルシャなどがいる。

平日の夕方はとくに混んでいないようだが、土日は混雑する。小さな子どもも歓迎だ。木曜日は"メンズデー"となっていて、男性客は200円引き。

Data Box

Resident animals 店内にいる動物	cats	猫
Station 最寄駅	Oimachi	大井町
Cover charge 基本料金	1,000 yen for one hour; 1,200 yen for one hour on weekends and holidays	1時間1,000円　土日祝日は1時間1,200円
Open hours 営業時間	11am-9pm	11:00～21:00
Address 住所	Shinagawa-ku, Higashi-Oi 5-7-14 [3 minutes from Oimachi station (Keihin Tohoku, Rinkai, Tokyu Oimachi lines)]	品川区東大井5-7-14 [大井町駅から徒歩3分（京浜東北線、臨海線、東急大井町線）]
Cafe menu カフェメニュー	coffee, tea and soft drinks	コーヒー、紅茶、ソフトドリンク
Animal treats 動物のおやつ	cat snacks 150 yen	猫のおやつ 150円

Website: http://www.catcafe-marumaru.net/　　　Phone: 03-5715-6118

Neko no Te
Chiba

"Hand of the Cat" is one of the most casual cat cafes we've ever been. When we asked how many animals were in residence, we were told the number was around fifteen or twenty, as if it was simply impossible to keep an accurate count. And indeed during the hour we were there, cats we had never seen before would occasionally slip in from other, hidden rooms, stake out a comfortable spot and proceed to take a nap. It's that kind of place.

Occupying a very lived-in former residential apartment, the public part of the cafe contains two connected playrooms and a small entrance area where arriving visitors wash their hands and exchange their shoes for cat slippers. We recommend you opt for the Harem Set—it gets you one hour of cat time, plus an iced cafe latte or other drink, and a decent-sized plate of cat snacks.

The snack plate, a pile of boiled chicken cut up into bite-sized strips, is presented to you with some fanfare as the staff member bangs on the side of the plate with a spoon. After that you're free to distribute morsels of chicken as you see fit to the suddenly attentive crowd.

After snacking, many of the cats like to return to their naps, so make the most of the attention while you can. We made friends with a very outgoing Sphynx cat, but most of the other residents seemed content to receive snacks and pose for photos. The best time for cat interaction is probably first thing in the morning when the cafe opens.

Overall: ☕☕☕☕☕
総合評価

Visitor amenities: ☕☕☕☕
店内設備

Animal interactivity: ☕☕☕
動物とのふれあい

猫の手

千葉

〈猫の手〉ほど、ざっくばらんな店はあまりないだろう。店内に猫は何匹いるのかとたずねたところ、15匹から20匹ぐらいだが、正確な数は分からないとの答えだった。私たちが店内にいると、見たことのない猫が別の部屋からそっと入り込んできて、気持ちのよい場所を確保するとそのまま寝てしまうような、そんな雰囲気の店だ。

以前は人が住んでいたアパートの一室にあり、共用のカフェに隣接して、2つの部屋をつなげたプレイルームと、来店者が手を洗い、猫スリッパに履きかえる狭い受付エリアがある。猫ハーレムセットがおすすめだ。1時間猫と過ごせるし、アイスカフェラテなどの飲み物と、ボリューム満点の猫のおやつがついてくる。

猫のおやつは一口大に細かくカットされたゆで鶏だが、スタッフが皿をスプーンでたたいてファンファーレとともに運んできてくれる。その後は、急にそわそわしだした猫たちに、好きなように与えることができる。

おやつのあとは、ほとんどの猫がまた寝てしまうので、できるだけ引きつけておいたほうがよい。私たちはとても元気のよいスフィンクスと仲良くなることができたが、他の猫たちはほとんど、おやつをもらって写真を撮ると満足してしまうみたいだ。猫とふれあいたかったら、店が開店する朝一番がベストだろう。

Data Box

Resident animals 店内にいる動物	cats	猫
Station 最寄駅	Kashiwa	柏
Cover charge 基本料金	600 yen for 30 minutes, 800 yen for one hour. Harem set 1,400 yen for one hour with one drink and cat snack	30分 600円 1時間 800円 ハーレムセット1時間 1400円ワンドリンクと猫のおやつ付き
Open hours 営業時間	11:30am-8pm; 10am-8pm weekends and holidays	11:30〜20:00 土日祝日は 10:00〜20:00
Address 住所	Chiba-ken, Kashiwa-shi 3-7-21, Shiina Bldg. 401 [4 minutes from Kashiwa station (Tobu line)]	千葉県柏市 3-7-21 椎名ビル 401 [柏駅 (JR線、東武線) から徒歩4分]
Cafe menu カフェメニュー	coffee, tea and soft drinks from 400 yen, meals from 700 yen	コーヒー、お茶、ソフトドリンク 400円から、食事は700円から
Animal treats 動物のおやつ	cat snacks 200 yen	猫用スナック 200円

Website: http://www.nekote.jp/   Phone: 04-7168-8629

Neko JaLaLa
Akihabara

JaLaLa distinguish themselves within the competitive cat-cafe world with their choice of exotic breeds such as Abyssinians and Maine Coons—seventeen in all, including some of the largest housecats we've ever encountered. The long-running shop consists of a smallish playroom that's amply furnished with numerous perches, shelves and feline-friendly enclosures.

Although the cats here seem to be as bored with visitors as usual, they changed their attitude when we bribed them with tuna, and they were soon eating out of our hands. The 350-yen cat snack (a reasonably hefty helping of tuna) is a good investment if you want a more interactive experience. Floor-based ping pong is another popular pastime.

Staff are friendly and enthusiastic, and they will provide English-speaking visitors with a book introducing all the cats, who for some reason each have their own email address. (We haven't investigated whether or not they write back.) The usual animal cafe rules apply—no flash photos, no roughhousing, and let sleeping cats lie.

There's a one-drink minimum on top of the cover charge. Coffee, tea and beer are served, starting at 350 yen for an iced oolong tea.

Overall: ☕☕☕☕☕
総合評価

Visitor amenities: ☕☕
店内設備

Animal interactivity: ☕☕☕
動物とのふれあい

ねこ JaLaLa

秋葉原

〈ねこ JaLaLa〉は、アビシニアンやメインクーンなどの珍しい品種をそろえていて、競争の激しい猫カフェ業界でも目立つ存在だ。総勢17匹の猫がいるが、なかには見たこともないような大きなイエネコもいた。細長い形をしたこの店には、小さめのプレイルームがあって、たくさんの猫用止まり木、棚や、猫に配慮したフェンスが設置してある。

他の店同様、ここの猫も客には飽き飽きしているようだが、私たちがツナを取り出すと態度が一変して、あっと言う間になくなってしまった。350円の猫のおやつ（ツナがたくさん入っている）は、猫たちともっとふれあいたいのなら買っておいて損はない。床でピンポン玉をころがしてやるのも面白い。

熱心で親切なスタッフが、英語を話す客向けに猫たち全員を紹介した冊子をくれるのだが、それぞれの猫のメールアドレスがなぜか記載してある（返信があるのかどうか、まだ試していない）。他の動物カフェと気をつけることは同じだ。フラッシュ撮影は禁止。大きな声は出さないように。寝ている猫を起こすのはやめよう。

基本料金以外にも、最低ワンドリンク注文しなければならない。350円のウーロン茶から、コーヒー、お茶、ビールまでいろいろある。

🕐 Data Box

Resident animals 店内にいる動物	cats	猫
Station 最寄駅	Akihabara	秋葉原
Cover charge 基本料金	530 yen for 30 minutes, 1,010 yen for one hour (1,060 yen on weekends and holidays), plus drink order	30分 530円　1時間 1,010円（土日祝日 1,060円）　他に飲み物の注文が必要
Open hours 営業時間	11am-8pm (last admission 7:30pm)	11:00～20:00（最終入場 19:30）
Address 住所	Chiyoda-ku, Soto-Kanda 3-5-5 1F [3 minutes from Suehirocho station (Ginza line); 6 minutes from Akihabara station (JR line)]	千代田区外神田 3-5-5-1F［末広町駅（銀座線）から徒歩3分、秋葉原駅(JR線)から徒歩6分］
Cafe menu カフェメニュー	coffee, tea and soft drinks from 350 yen, beer from 550 yen	コーヒー、お茶、ソフトドリンク 350円から　ビール 550円から
Animal treats 動物のおやつ	cat snack 350 yen	猫用スナック 350円

Website: http://www.nekojalala.com/　　　Phone: 03-3258-2525

Neko no Kanzume
Nakano

A relatively small neighborhood establishment, "Can of Cats" is noteworthy for their very playful cats, and human staff who go out of their way to keep them entertained with a full complement of cat toys and a lot of energy. Unlike most cafes, you're allowed to pick up and hold the animals here in addition to petting them—the staff will tell you which ones enjoy it and which are off-limits.

Easy chairs and ottomans here are fairly comfortable, although the chairs tend to be occupied by sleepy felines. Cat furniture is more elaborate than average, with numerous well-used climbing towers, perches and cubbyholes. There are fifteen cats and kittens in all, so there's always some activity, and occasionally a bit of drama, although staff are quick to quell any disturbances.

The cover charge includes a soft drink, and you can help yourself to a bottle from the fridge. Cat snacks are included in the price too.

The cafe is located up two flights of stairs in a small office building alongside the Nakano Broadway complex. Ring the doorbell when you reach the third floor.

Overall: ☕☕☕☕☕
総合評価

Visitor amenities: ☕☕☕
店内設備

Animal interactivity: ☕☕☕☕
動物とのふれあい

ねこの缶づめ
中野

比較的小規模で、地域密着型の〈ねこの缶づめ〉は、いたずら好きの猫たちと、猫のおもちゃを総動員してエネルギッシュに猫をじゃれさせている、人間のスタッフのいる店だ。他のカフェと違って、なでるだけでなく、好きな猫を選んでだっこすることができる。スタッフがだっこされるのが好きな猫や、やめておいたほうがよい猫を教えてくれる。

ここのひじ掛け椅子やオットマンはとても快適なのだが、眠っている猫たちに独占されることもしばしば。猫用の家具が充実していて、よく使いこまれた猫タワーや、止まり木、小さな穴の開いている猫用の家などがたくさん置いてある。総勢15匹ほどの猫や子猫がいる。いつもにぎやかで、時には猫同士で喧嘩になることもあるが、スタッフが素早くなだめてくれる。

基本料金にはソフトドリンク代が含まれていて、冷蔵庫から自分でペットボトルを一本とる。料金には猫のおやつ代も含まれている。

中野ブロードウェイの並びにある小さなオフィスビルの3階が店舗となっている。3階まで上ったら、インターホンを鳴らそう。

Data Box

Resident animals 店内にいる動物	cats	猫
Station 最寄駅	Nakano	中野
Cover charge 基本料金	1,000 yen for one hour, 1,200 yen on weekends, with one drink.	1 時間 1,000 円　土日祝日は 1,200 円　ワンドリンク付き
Open hours 営業時間	1pm-8pm; 11am-8pm on weekends and holidays. Closed Wednesdays and Thursdays	13:00～20:00　土日祝日 11:00～20:00　水曜、木曜定休
Address 住所	Nakano-ku, Nakano 5-68-9 AK Bldg. 3F [3 minutes from Nakano station North Exit (JR and Tozai lines)]	中野区中野 5-68-9 AK ビル 3F [中野駅 (JR 線、東西線) 北口から徒歩 3 分]
Cafe menu カフェメニュー	bottled soft drinks	ペットボトル飲料
Animal treats 動物のおやつ	cat snacks (included in cover)	猫のおやつ　猫用スナック（基本料金に含まれている）

Website: http://www.nekonokanzume.com/　　　Phone: 070-6522-2225

Cateriam

Shimo-Kitazawa

With its spacious, comfortable lounge area, Cateriam is a pleasant place to relax over tea and scones or a glass of wine. While there are only a few perches, the room is well furnished with cardboard boxes, baskets and large pots for the resident cats to curl up in. Most seating is on the floor (on cushions), with a large-size sofa in one corner.

When you enter you'll be asked how long you expect to stay—the basic pack is sixty minutes and includes a soft drink, although you can opt for a fifteen- or thirty-minute test pack if you just want to check out the place out quickly.

Although the space is relatively large there are only eleven resident cats—most of them sleeping at any given time—so cat interactions can be a bit limited during busy times such as weekends.

The breeds here include American Shorthair, Chinchilla Persian, and Maine Coon.

Overall: ☕☕☕☕☕
総合評価

Visitor amenities: ☕☕☕
店内設備

Animal interactivity: ☕☕☕
動物とのふれあい

キャテリアム

下北沢

広々とした快適なラウンジがある〈キャテリアム〉はお茶とスコーン、もしくはワインを一杯飲みながらくつろげる、心地よい場所だ。室内に猫用の止まり木は2、3個しかないものの、猫が中に入って丸くなれる段ボール箱、かご、土鍋などがたくさん置いてある。床に腰を下ろすことになるが（クッションがある）、部屋の隅に大きなソファがひとつ置いてある。

入店時に滞在時間を選べる。基本パックは60分ソフトドリンク付きだが、店をさっとチェックしたいだけなら、15分か30分のお試しパックを選ぶことができる。

店内のスペースは比較的広いものなのに、猫は11匹しかいない。どの時間帯もほとんど寝ている。土日などの混雑時には、猫とあまりふれあえない可能性もある。

アメリカンショートヘア、チンチラ・ペルシャ、メインクーンなどがいる。

🕐 Data Box

Resident animals 店内にいる動物	cats	猫
Station 最寄駅	Shimo-Kitazawa	下北沢
Cover charge 基本料金	Basic pack is 1,000 yen for one hour with one soft drink. Test pack is 15 minutes for 300 yen or 30 minutes for 500 yen without a drink	1時間ワンドリンク付き 1,000円　お試しパック 15分 300円 30分 500円（ドリンクなし）
Open hours 営業時間	11am-9pm; 10am-9:30pm on weekends. Closed Mondays	11:00～21:00（土日は 10:00～21:30）月曜定休
Address 住所	Setagaya-ku, Kitazawa 2-26-6, Mont Blanc Bldg 2F [2 minutes from Shimo-Kitazawa station (Odakyu and Inokashira lines)]	世田谷区北沢 2-26-6 モンブランビル 2F ［下北沢駅（小田急線、井の頭線）から徒歩 2分］
Cafe menu カフェメニュー	coffee and tea 300 yen, beer 450 yen, cakes from 300 yen, fried noodles 850 yen.	コーヒー、お茶 300円　ビール 450円　ケーキ 300円から　焼きそば 850円
Animal treats 動物のおやつ	None	なし

Website: http://cateriam.com/　　　　Phone: 03-3468-8114

Nekorobi
Ikebukuro

One of Tokyo's oldest cat cafes, Nekorobi is a friendly, relaxed spot to hang out, although it's a lot better when it's not crowded, as there are only eleven resident cats to go around. You'll find the usual collection of cat toys, climbing trees, hideaway spots and cardboard boxes, along with low-rise, cat-level seats around the periphery of the room.

In addition to feline entertainment, there are a few games to play as well as Japanese-language manga and magazines. A large-screen TV in one corner plays a slide show of cat pictures from the cafe's history dating back to 2008. The three staff members are friendly, and very accustomed to foreign visitors.

During our visit on a weekday afternoon we had to wait five minutes to get in, and about 80% of the visitors were tourist families and student groups. Unfortunately, it was catnap time and the cats must not be disturbed, so customers are forced to make their own entertainment. People were sprawled about on the floor playing cards, waiting longingly and expectantly for some cats to wake up. They eventually did, but only to stretch, turn around and go back to sleep.

The minimum stay is sixty minutes, and that includes all you can drink from the vending machine. Remember to put a lid on your drink, as some of the cats love to play a friendly game of Knock over the Drinks on the Table.

Among the familiar Maine Coon, Chinchilla Golden, Munchkin, and Exotic Shorthair breeds, there are also some more unusual Scottish Fold and Somali cats, which look very cute when they're asleep. Cat feeding times are at 11am and 8:30pm.

Overall: ☕☕☕☕
総合評価

Visitor amenities: ☕☕☕
店内設備

Animal interactivity: ☕☕
動物とのふれあい

ねころび

池袋

　東京の猫カフェのなかでも古くからある〈ねころび〉は気軽にゆっくりくつろげる場所だが、店内に猫は11匹しかいないので混雑時は避けたほうがよい。おなじみの猫のおもちゃ、キャットタワー、隠れ場所や、段ボール箱があり、猫目線の低い椅子が壁側に配置してある。

　猫とのお楽しみ以外にも、いくつかゲームも置いてあるし、日本語のマンガや雑誌もある。部屋の隅にある大画面のテレビは2008年からの店の歴代の猫たちをスライドショーで映し出している。3人いるスタッフは親切で、外国人の客にも慣れている。

　平日の午後に訪れたところ、入店に5分待たねばならず、店内の客の8割は家族連れの観光客か、学生のグループだった。運悪く、ちょうど猫が寝ている時間で静かにしていなければならなかったので、客は各自で暇つぶしをするしかなかった。室内の思い思いの場所に座ってトランプをしたりしながら、猫が起きるのを今か今かと待っていた。やがて猫が起きてきたが、伸びをすると丸くなり、結局また寝てしまった。

　滞在できる時間は1時間から。飲み物のサーバーがあって、フリードリンクとなっている。「テーブルの上の飲み物ころがし」ゲームが好きな猫もいるので、飲み物には必ずフタをつけよう。

　よく見かけるメインクーン、チンチラゴールデン、マンチカン、エキゾチックショートヘアの他にも、ちょっと変わったスコティッシュフォールドやソマリ（寝顔がとてもかわいい）もいる。猫の食事タイムは午前11時と午後8時半だ。

🕐 Data Box

Resident animals 店内にいる動物	cats	猫
Station 最寄駅	Ikebukuro	池袋
Cover charge 基本料金	1,100 yen for one hour with free drinks, 1,300 yen on weekends and holidays	1時間 1,100円フリードリンク付き　土日祝日は1,300円
Open hours 営業時間	11am-10pm	11:00～22:00
Address 住所	Toshima-ku, Higashi-Ikebukuro 1-28-1, Tact T-O Bldg. 3F [5 minutes from Ikebukuro station (JR, Tobu, Yurakucho lines)]	豊島区東池袋1-28-1 タクトT・Oビル3F［池袋駅(JR線、東武線、有楽町線など)から徒歩5分］
Cafe menu カフェメニュー	unlimited soft drinks included	多種類のソフトドリンクが料金に含まれている
Animal treats 動物のおやつ	none	なし

Website: http://www.nekorobi.jp/

Phone: 03-6228-0646

Nekobukuro
Ikebukuro

While it's not strictly a cat cafe, Cat's House Nekobukuro on the eighth floor of Tokyu Hands in Ikebukuro is the oldest cat petting zoo in town. It's been open since 2000 and draws a crowd of tourists and regulars with its reasonable price, Pee-wee's Playhouse design and plentiful cats.

The theme seems to be a surreal mix of cats, trains and kindergarten. You enter through the left-hand door into a fake train station with a parked train carriage full of sleeping cats. There are two other rooms decorated with overhead walkways for cats, toy cases mounted perpendicularly on walls, and a few wooden chairs for tired visitors.

There are about forty different cats on call at the park, and typically about twelve to fifteen cats on duty at any particular time. While a few were curled up in baskets asleep, many were actively trotting around the walkways above our heads, or darting through secret cat doors in the walls.

All your favorite breeds are represented, including American Shorthair, Maine Coon, Scottish Fold, Munchkin, American Curl, Bengal and Ragdoll.

After you've paid your entry fee there's no time limit other than your own bladder (there's no bathroom inside the facility, and no reentry). The usual cat cafe rules apply—disinfect your hands upon entering and leaving the room, don't wake sleeping cats, and don't chase cats around.

Overall: ☕☕☕☕
総合評価

Visitor amenities: ☕☕
店内設備

Animal interactivity: ☕☕
動物とのふれあい

ねこぶくろ

池袋

　厳密には猫カフェではないのだが、〈Cat's House ねこぶくろ〉は東急ハンズ池袋店の8階にあり、都内でも古くからある動物とふれあえる場所だ。手ごろな値段や、カラフルな店内、たくさんの猫たちが2000年のオープン以来、多くの観光客やリピーターを引きつけている。

　店内は猫と電車と幼稚園をミックスしたような奇抜な雰囲気になっている。左開きになっているドアを開けて店内に入ると、電車の駅があって、車内にはたくさん猫が寝ている。他にも2部屋あり、人間の頭上を猫が歩けるように通路が作ってあって、おもちゃ箱が壁側に重ねて積み上げてある。客が休憩するための木製の椅子もいくつか置いてある。

　店内には40匹の猫が待機していて、常時12〜15匹の猫たちとふれあえる。かごの中で寝ている猫も何匹かいるが、多くは頭上の通り道を走ったり、壁にある秘密のドアを通りぬけたりしている。

　アメリカンショートヘア、メインクーン、スコティッシュフォールド、マンチカン、アメリカンカール、ベンガル、ラグドールなど、人気の品種をそろえている。

　入場料を払えば、トイレに行きたくなるまではいつまでもいられる（店内にトイレはなく、再入場はできない）。入るときと帰るときは手を消毒する、寝ている猫は起こさない、猫を追い回さないなど、基本的なルールは他の猫カフェと同じだ。

Data Box

Resident animals 店内にいる動物	cats	猫
Station 最寄駅	Ikebukuro	池袋
Cover charge 基本料金	600 yen; no re-entry	600円　再入場不可
Open hours 営業時間	10am-8pm	10:00〜20:00
Address 住所	Toshima-ku, Higashi-Ikebukuro 1-28-10, Tokyu Hands 8F [7 minutes from Ikebukuro station (JR, Tobu, Yurakucho lines)]	豊島区東池袋1-28-10 東急ハンズ8F［池袋駅（JR線、東武線、有楽町線など）から徒歩7分］
Cafe menu カフェメニュー	none	なし
Animal treats 動物のおやつ	none	なし

Website: http://www.p2-pet.com/nekobukuro/　　　Phone: 03-3980-6111

Neko no Mise
Machida

Run by a cat-welfare organization, Neko no Mise is a pleasant and reasonably priced place to drop by for a short coffee break or a relaxing afternoon. There are plenty of comfortable seats in the spacious playroom, and the cover charge is calculated in ten-minute increments for short visits, as well as economical three-hour plans. Drink orders are optional, and you can even bring your own lunch bento.

If you're in for the long haul, there's an option for unlimited soft drinks (coffee, tea, soda) from the vending machine for just 350 yen. A lot of visitors seem to be just hanging out—surfing the internet or reading as well as playing with more than 15 resident cats. The bookshelves are filled with hundreds of books, magazines and comics for your perusal, and at least one computer is available for visitors, in addition to free WiFi.

There are also lots of cat toys if you want to play with the cats, and cat snacks (300 yen) if you really want to make friends. Feeding times are listed as 12:30pm and 9:30pm—the best time to see the largest number of cats awake from their naps.

The cafe is located very close to Machida JR station, on the underdeveloped south side of the station. We almost missed it, as it's located in a nondescript building that seemed to be under renovation when we visited.

Overall: ☕☕☕☕☕
総合評価

Visitor amenities: ☕☕☕☕
店内設備

Animal interactivity: ☕☕
動物とのふれあい

猫喫茶　ねこのみせ

町田

猫の福祉団体によって運営されている〈ねこのみせ〉は気持ちのよい場所で、料金も安く、短いコーヒーブレイクや、ゆったりしたい午後にうってつけの店だ。広々としたプレイルームには座り心地のよい席がいくつも用意してあるし、基本料金は短い時間なら10分ごとの計算だ。お得な3時間のプランもある。飲み物はオプションとなるが、食べ物の持ち込みもできる。

もし長居するつもりなら、350円でドリンクサーバーからソフトドリンク（コーヒー、お茶、炭酸飲料）が飲み放題だ。客の大半は15〜18匹いる猫たちと遊ぶだけでなく、ネットサーフィンや、読書をしていて、くつろぎに来ているみたいだ。本棚には本、雑誌、マンガがぎっしりつまっていて読むことができるし、自由に使えるパソコンがが1台設置してある。Wi-Fi接続も無料。

猫と遊びたいのならおもちゃがたくさんあるし、もっと仲良くなりたければ猫のおやつが300円で買える。食事タイムは午後12時半と、午後9時半となっていて、一度にたくさんの猫たちが起き出してくるベストタイミングだ。

店はJR町田駅からほど近く駅南の、開発が進んでいない地域にある。改装中とおぼしき何の変哲もないビルに入っているので、危うく見逃すところだった。

Data Box

Resident animals 店内にいる動物	cats	猫
Station 最寄駅	Machida	町田
Cover charge 基本料金	150 yen for every ten minutes, or 1,500 yen for two hours	10分ごとに150円、もしくは2時間1,500円
Open hours 営業時間	Noon-10pm; 11am-10pm on weekends and holidays	12:00〜22:00　土日祝日は11:00〜22:00
Address 住所	Machida-shi, Hara-Machida 1-2-9-202 [2 minutes from Machida station Central Exit (JR line)]	町田市原町田1-2-9-202　[町田駅（JR線、小田急線）中央出口から徒歩2分]
Cafe menu カフェメニュー	unlimited soft drinks 350 yen	多種類のソフトドリンク 350円
Animal treats 動物のおやつ	cat snacks 300 yen	猫用スナック 300円

Website: http://nya-n.jp/　　　　　**Phone:** 042-722-0544

Neko no Jikan Kita-honten

Osaka Tenjinbashi

Maybe it was just a matter of the time of day we were there, but Time for Cats seems like one of the sleepiest cat cafes we've ever visited. Main activities here seem to be a) napping, and b) scouting out locations for upcoming naps. There was a flurry of activity when one cat drank some water, but that was about it—overall it was a very relaxing experience, and we began to feel a bit sleepy ourselves.

Fortunately our admission fee included a cup of coffee at the adjacent cafe, called Holy Land, which is equipped with windows looking onto the cat playroom. Holy Land often has a friendly dog in residence, and they're open well into the evening, when they serve wine (Chilean wine Gato Negro) and a light cafe food menu.

In operation since March 2004, Time for Cats claims to be Japan's oldest cat cafe and currently has eighteen resident felines. Among the exotic breeds are a Burmese, a Japanese Bobtail, and a cross between an American Shorthair and a Bengal, as well as many Munchkins, Ragdolls, and Shorthairs. The website has a rather poignant photo page of "gone but not forgotten" previous residents.

Overall: ☕☕☕☕☕
総合評価

Visitor amenities: ☕☕☕☕
店内設備

Animal interactivity: ☕☕
動物とのふれあい

猫の時間　きた本店
大阪　天神橋

おそらく入店した時間が悪かったのだろうが、〈猫の時間〉は、これまで行ったなかでもとても眠たげな店だった。ここの主な活動は、a）寝ている、b）寝る場所を探している、のどちらかという具合だ。一匹水を飲みに行くと少し動きがあるが、それだけだ。おかげで、私たちもちょっと眠くなってしまった。

幸いなことに、入場料には隣接したカフェ、"Holy Land" でのコーヒーが一杯ついていた。猫のプレイルームを窓からのぞくことができる。このカフェには人なつこい犬が一匹いて、遅くまで営業しているが、夜はワイン（「ガトー・ネグロ」という、黒猫がトレードマークのチリワイン）と、軽食を頼むことができる。

2004年3月にオープンした〈猫の時間〉は、日本ではじめて誕生した猫カフェだということだ。現在は18匹の猫がいる。珍しい品種では、マンチカン、ラグドール、ショートヘアの他にバーミーズ、ジャパニーズボブテイル、アメリカンショートヘアとベンガルとの交配種がいる。ホームページには、「いつまでも忘れない」、以前店にいた猫たちの写真のページがあり、ちょっとしんみりする。

🕐 Data Box

Resident animals 店内にいる動物	cats	ネコ
Station 最寄駅	Tenjinbashi	天神橋
Cover charge 基本料金	1,100 yen for one hour with one drink, 1,200 yen on weekends and holidays	1時間ワンドリンク付き1,100円 土日祝日は1,200円
Open hours 営業時間	11am-9pm; 11am-7pm Mondays; 10am-7pm Sundays and holidays	11:00 〜 21:00　月曜日 11:00 〜 19:00　日曜祝日 10:00 〜 19:00
Address 住所	Osaka-shi, Kita-ku, Kurosakicho 5-16, HEART Bldg. 2F [5 minutes from Tenjinbashi station (JR line)]	大阪市北区黒崎町 5-16 HEART ビル 2F　［天神橋駅（JR線）から徒歩 5 分］
Cafe menu カフェメニュー	coffee, tea, soft drinks	コーヒー、お茶、ソフトドリンク
Animal treats 動物のおやつ	cat treats available	猫のおやつあり

Website: http://www.nekonojikan.com/kitahonten/　　Phone: 06-6359-3700

Nekobiyaka
Himeji

Yes, it's the world's first and only black-cat cafe, located near Himeji's central station and along the route to the town's famous landmark castle. While there were only six cats present when we visited (the website lists a dozen), they were an extremely lively bunch—running around, jumping in the air, and playing a vigorous game of fetch with a cloth-covered toy. We're not sure, but we suspect that catnip may have been involved.

Since it's hard to tell the cats here apart, they all wear different-colored bandanas around their necks, and their names incorporate their identifying color. The staff will lend you a little book with photos of all the cats, listing their names and birthdays.

The cafe is attractively furnished in residential living-room style, with windows looking out onto one of Himeji's shopping streets. Background music is an odd mix of easy-listening and music-box arrangements of pop songs. Coffee and other soft drinks are 400 yen (we had a very nice iced cappuccino), while alcoholic beverages start at 600 yen. Cat treats are not available, however.

Overall: ☕☕☕☕☕
総合評価

Visitor amenities: ☕☕☕☕
店内設備

Animal interactivity: ☕☕
動物とのふれあい

cat cafe ねこびやか

姫路

そう、ここは世界で唯一の黒猫カフェだ。姫路駅からほど近く、町の名所となっている姫路城へ向かう途中にある。私たちが入店したときは6匹しかいなかったが(ホームページには10匹あまり紹介されている)、とても元気な猫たちで、走り回ったり、飛び跳ねたり、ぬいぐるみを取って来る遊びをしたりしていた。猫を元気にするキャットニップ入りのぬいぐるみを使っているのかもしれないと思った。

どの猫も見分けがつかないので、それぞれ違う色のバンダナを首に巻いていて、その色が入った名前がつけられている。スタッフが、猫全員の写真と名前、生年月日が書いてある本を貸してくれるだろう。

店内はリビングルームのように家具が配置されている。窓からは姫路の商店街が見下ろせる。BGMはイージー・リスニング音楽と、ポップソングをオルゴール演奏したものをとりまぜたちょっと変わったものだ。コーヒーと他のソフトドリンクは400円だ（私たちが頼んだカプチーノはおいしかった）。アルコール類は600円から。猫のおやつはない。

Data Box

Resident animals 店内にいる動物	black cats	黒猫
Station 最寄駅	Himeji	姫路
Cover charge 基本料金	1,000 yen for one hour	1時間 1,000 円
Open hours 営業時間	Noon-9pm; Noon-7pm Sundays; last admission one hour before closing. Closed Tuesdays	12:00～21:00 日曜は12:00～19:00 最終入場は閉店1時間前 火曜定休
Address 住所	Hyogo-ken, Himeji-shi, Ekimaecho 322, Mifune Bldg. 2F [5 minutes from Himeji station (Sanyo line)]	兵庫県姫路市駅前町322ミフネビル2F ［姫路駅（JR山陽本線）から徒歩5分］
Cafe menu カフェメニュー	soft drinks 400 yen, alcoholic beverages 600 yen	ソフトドリンク400円 アルコール飲料600円
Animal treats 動物のおやつ	none	なし

Website: http://nekobiyaka.jugem.jp/   Phone: 090-6757-2810

And a few more animals....

Dog Heart from Aquamarine

Yoyogi Hachiman

A pack of happy, tail-wagging pups greeted us in boisterous fashion upon our arrival at Dog Heart, letting us know that we'd be in for a lively afternoon at one of Tokyo's more gregarious animal cafes. Unlike the often reserved residents of your typical cat cafe, the sixteen dogs here are just thrilled to have human visitors and they aren't shy about letting you know it.

After you check in and wash your hands you'll be issued an apron to protect your street clothes. Please note that unsecured apron strings may be mistaken for chew toys. There's one large sofa, but if that's occupied by other visitors you can stretch out on cushions on the floor.

Wherever you choose to sit, friendly dogs will come to you to be petted, initiate games of fetch, or take a snooze in your lap. If you want to take a break, next to the playroom is a small, dogless cafe area where you can help yourself to tea, soda or juice for 100 yen a drink.

On our most recent visit, the canine staff comprised a pack of toy poodles, beagles and a lone golden retriever. Should you want to get some fresh air and exercise (and if you don't mind performing clean-up duties), you can take one of the dogs out for a walk in nearby Yoyogi Park—just choose the "dog rental" option when you check in.

DOG HEART from アクアマリン　　代々木八幡

　〈DOG HEART from アクアマリン〉に入ると、うれしそうにしっぽを振った子犬の群れが元気よく出迎えてくれた。首都圏の動物カフェのなかでも、動物と活発に遊べるタイプのここなら、楽しい午後を過ごせそうな予感がした。たいていはよそよそしい態度をとる猫カフェの猫たちと違って、ここの16匹の犬たちは人間の客が来ると大喜びで、その気持ちを素直に表現してくれる。
　受付を済ませて手を洗ったら、私服を汚れから守るエプロンが渡される。エプロンの紐が垂れていると、噛むおもちゃと勘違いされるので要注意だ。大きなソファがひとつあるが、先客がいたら、床のクッションに座ることができる。
　どこにいても、人なつこい犬たちがなでてもらいに来たり、物を放りなげて取って来る遊びを始めたり、膝の上で居眠りしたりする。疲れたら、プレイルームの隣には、犬は入れないカフェエリアがある。お茶やソーダ、ジュースがセルフサービスで100円だ。
　前回訪れたときは何匹かのトイプードル、ビーグルと一匹のゴールデンレトリバーからなる犬スタッフがいた。外の新鮮な空気を吸い、運動したくなったら（フンの後始末もできるのなら）、一匹連れ出して近所の代々木公園を散歩できる。「ドッグレンタル」のオプションを受付でチェックしよう。

Overall:
総合評価

Visitor amenities: ☕☕
店内設備

Animal interactivity: ☕☕☕☕
動物とのふれあい

🕐 Data Box

Resident animals 店内にいる動物	dogs	犬
Station 最寄駅	Yoyogi-Hachiman	代々木八幡
Cover charge 基本料金	950 yen for 30 minutes, 1,550 yen for one hour in the cafe. Dog rental charges start from 3,600 yen per hour	カフェ内30分950円、1時間1,550円　ドッグレンタルは1時間3,600円から
Open hours 営業時間	11am-7pm	11:00～19:00
Address 住所	Shibuya-ku, Tomigaya 1-45-2, Y's Park Bldg 2F [5 minutes from Yoyogi-Hachiman station (Odakyu Odawara line)]	渋谷区富ヶ谷1丁目45-2 Y'sパークビル2F［代々木八幡駅（小田急小田原線）から徒歩5分］
Cafe menu カフェメニュー	soft drinks 100 yen	各種ソフトドリンク100円
Animal treats 動物のおやつ	none	なし

Website: http://dog-heart.ico.bz/　　　　Phone: 03-3469-4115

フクロウ・タカ etc.

Owls, Hawks

Hawkeye
Oshiage

Billed as a "raptorial photo and snack bar," Hawkeye offers a couple dozen raptors—hawks and falcons as well as owls—for visitor photo sessions. These include pictures with the nearby Tokyo Skytree in the background (for an extra 500 yen), and you can even borrow a tripod if you need one.

You can also pet a few of the birds—we had a pleasant session with a barn owl who really enjoyed having his neck rubbed. Be sure to ask the staff which ones are safe to touch, though. We were informed that one usually friendly bird was feeling a bit moody because he was molting.

We arrived just before feeding time (around 4pm), and it was a vivid reminder that these birds are carnivorous—the owner dispensed chunks of raw meat, which were caught by the birds in midair. The owner first became interested in owls and hawks after encountering them through his hobby of paragliding, and now he raises them from hatchlings and obviously has quite a bit of affection for them. The species here include Harris's hawk, buzzard, Eurasian eagle-owl, spotted eagle-owl and European scops owl.

The shop is divided into a cafe area—where you can order coffee and tea, beer and snacks—and two big bird rooms (referred to as "raptor booths") visible from the cafe through glass walls. You can choose to just be an observer from the cafe zone or inside the bird room, or for an extra fee, handle the birds.

If you want to reserve a spot you can do so by email at hawkeye@takanome.info.

Overall: ☕☕☕☕☕☕☕
総合評価

Visitor amenities: ☕☕☕☕☕
店内設備

Animal interactivity: ☕☕☕☕
動物とのふれあい

鷹乃眼

押上

「猛禽類の写真とスナック・バー」をかかげる〈鷹乃眼〉には、フクロウのみならず、鷹やハヤブサなどの猛禽類が20羽あまりいて、一緒に写真が撮れる。近くの東京スカイツリーを背景にした撮影も可能（追加料金500円）。必要なら三脚も貸してくれる。

　さわれる鳥もいる。私たちは首をこすってやると気持ちよさそうにしていたメンフクロウと楽しい時間を過ごすことができた。さわってもよい鳥をスタッフに確認するのを忘れないように。いつもは人なつこいのだが、羽が生え変わる時期で少々機嫌が悪い鳥がいるとその日は教えてもらった。

　食事タイム（午後4時ごろ）の直前に入店したのだが、猛禽類が肉食だとあらためて気づかされた。オーナーが生肉の塊を放りなげると、鳥たちは空中でキャッチしたのだ。オーナーは趣味のパラグライダーでフクロウや鷹と出会い、興味を持つようになって、今ではヒナから育てているそうだ。鳥たちへの愛にあふれた人物だ。店には、ハリスホーク、ノスリ、ユーラシアンワシミミズク、アフリカワシミミズク、ヨーロッパコノハズクがいる。

　店はコーヒーやお茶、ビールや軽食を注文できるカフェエリアと、カフェからガラス越しに見ることができる、2つの大きな「猛禽類ブース」に分かれている。カフェで眺めるだけでもいいし、猛禽類ブースに入って追加料金を払えば、鳥にさわることができる。

　Eメールで予約可能。アドレスはhawkeye@takanome.info

Data Box

Resident animals 店内にいる動物	owls, hawks, falcons	フクロウ、鷹、ハヤブサ
Station 最寄駅	Oshiage	押上
Cover charge 基本料金	1,500 per hour with soft drink, 1,700 per hour with alcoholic beverage, and bird-handling in the raptor booth. 1,000 yen per hour with soft drink without bird handling	1時間 1,500円（ソフトドリンク付）1時間 1700円（アルコール飲料付）ふれあい部屋で鳥を腕に乗せることができる　鳥にさわらない場合は1時間 1000円（ソフトドリンク付）
Open hours 営業時間	1pm-7pm. Closed Mondays, Thursdays	13:00～19:00 月曜、木曜は定休日
Address 住所	Sumida-ku, Narihira 1-8-9 [5 minutes from Oshiage station (Asakusa line); 7 minutes from Tokyo Skytree station (Tobu Skytree line)]	墨田区業平 1-8-9 [押上駅（浅草線）から徒歩5分　とうきょうスカイツリー駅（東武スカイツリーライン）から徒歩7分]
Cafe menu カフェメニュー	soft drinks from 600 yen, beer from 1,000 yen in the cafe	カフェ内で、各種ソフトドリンク600円から　ビール 1000円から
Animal treats 動物のおやつ	none	なし

Website: http://1st.geocities.jp/takanomesky/　　　Phone: 090-2338-2558

BiBi & GeorGe
Kobe Motomachi

The cafe's good-natured staff and friendly birds make this a very pleasant place to spend an hour of your time. The setup is a bit unusual, starting with the ticket machine at the entrance of the three-story shop where you choose what you want to drink in the cafe and how long you want to stay.

The first floor has a resident bird or two, but it seems to be mainly an entrance lobby, or perhaps a waiting area during busy times. Up a narrow staircase on the second floor is the main cafe space, where you can relax and drink your coffee or soft drink (or beer) and recharge your batteries. This is also where you'll be briefed on the cafe's procedures and bird safety rules, with a written instruction sheet in English or Japanese.

The main aviary is up on the third floor, and this is where you can meet most of the seventeen resident birds. The big snowy owl down at the end of the room was quite a character, clowning around for photos and trying to peck at anyone who got within range of its beak. (The proprietor laughingly demonstrated this to us, and said that it didn't really hurt.) The baby owl on a skateboard was another popular model for photographs.

Most of the birds are pettable (gently and briefly on the head only), although a few are on break at any given time—the staff will tell you which ones not to touch. You can also ask the staff if you can hold one of the smaller birds, although it may depend on how crowded the place is.

Kobe's first owl cafe boasts unusual species such as the burrowing owl and western screech owl, along with the familiar eagle-owls, snowy owl, barn owl and tawny owl.

Overall: ☕☕☕☕☕☕☕
総合評価

Visitor amenities: ☕☕☕☕
店内設備

Animal interactivity: ☕☕☕☕
動物とのふれあい

ビビ＆ジョージ

神戸　元町

気さくなスタッフと、フレンドリーなフクロウたちのいる気持ちのよいこの店なら、充実した時間を過ごすことができるだろう。入店の流れがちょっと他とは違う。3フロアあるこの店の1階の受付でまずカフェでの飲み物と、滞在時間を選んで券売機でチケットを購入する。1階には、フクロウが1、2羽いるものの、エントランスロビーか、混雑時の待合室といった感じだ。狭い階段を上がると、2階はカフェスペースになっていて、コーヒーやソフトドリンク（ビールも）を飲んで、くつろいだり、電子機器の充電ができる。この部屋で、店の決まりや鳥の安全に関するルールについての説明を受ける。英語、もしくは日本語の説明書が渡される。

3階は鳥の部屋で、ここで店の17羽のフクロウたちのほとんどに会える。部屋の隅に面白い大きなシロフクロウがいて、写真を撮ろうとするとおどけてくれるし、近寄るともなく、くちばしでつつかれる（オーナーが笑いながらその様子を見せてくれたのだが、つつかれても痛くないそうだ）。スケボーに乗る子どものフクロウもいて、こちらも人気のある写真モデルだ。

ほとんどのフクロウをなでることができる（頭だけをやさしく、手短に）。どの時間帯も、休憩中のフクロウが一部いて、スタッフがさわらないように教えてくれる。小型のフクロウを腕に乗せてもよいかスタッフに聞くこともできるが、店の混雑具合によるだろう。

神戸初のフクロウカフェとなるこの店は、アナホリフクロウやニシアメリカオオコノハズクなどの珍しいフクロウがいる。他にも、おなじみのワシミミズク、シロフクロウ、メンフクロウ、モリフクロウもいる。

🕐 Data Box

Resident animals 店内にいる動物	owls	フクロウ
Station 最寄駅	Kobe Motomachi	元町
Cover charge 基本料金	1,000 for one hour with soft drink (1,200 with alcoholic beverage)	1時間1,000円ソフトドリンク付き（アルコール飲料付きは1,200円）
Open hours 営業時間	11am-8pm, last admission 7pm. Closed Mondays	11:00～20:00 最終入場 19:00 月曜定休
Address 住所	Kobe, Chuo-ku, Sakaemachi-dori 1-2-14, Umifuku Bldg 1-3F　[3 minutes from Motomachi station (JR and Hanshin lines)]	神戸市中央区栄町通1-2-14 海福ビル1F-3F [元町駅（JR線、阪神線）から徒歩3分]
Cafe menu カフェメニュー	free soft drink, beer, or chuhai	ソフトドリンクまたは、ビール、チューハイが料金に含まれている
Animal treats 動物のおやつ	none	なし

Website: http://kobefukuroucafe.com/　　**Phone:** 078-391-2960

Akiba Fukurou

Akihabara

This owl cafe in the center of Akihabara has a unique atmosphere—more like a theme-park attraction than an animal cafe. From the outside it looks like a repurposed downtown office, but inside it's a fantasy world of sleepy owls, crystal chandeliers, uniformed staff and soft classical music.

The cafe has been open since August 2014 and is popular with Japanese and tourists equally for its friendly vibe, high interactivity quotient and calming, relaxing atmosphere.

It's easy to make an online reservation, and once the date and time are confirmed you'll be asked to arrive ten minutes before the appointment. The uniformed staff hand out an informative folder (in Japanese and English) that goes well beyond the usual bird-handling etiquette tips. It also has pages of interesting info on owls' feeding habits, diet, eye color, pet laws, etc. Even the bird-handling talk is theatrical—while the manager makes the announcement, another staff member holds up a bird leash and shows how to return an owl to its perch—just like a flight attendant demonstrating a seat belt.

One dedicated customer confessed that she just couldn't bear to be away from the owls that day and had dropped by on her lunch break. She knew every one of the birds by name, and also gave us tips on their individual personalities. One first-timer sat at her table with a serene smile on her face as she stared enraptured at a little raptor perched on her arm. You could tell that she'd definitely be coming back soon.

The twenty resident owls are all very friendly and used to being handled.

Overall: ☕☕☕☕☕☕
総合評価

Visitor amenities: ☕☕☕☕☕
店内設備

Animal interactivity: ☕☕☕☕
動物とのふれあい

アキバフクロウ

秋葉原

　秋葉原の中心街にあるこの店は動物カフェというよりも、テーマパークのアトラクションのようで、独特の雰囲気だ。外観は商業地区の再利用店舗のようだが、中に入るとそこはファンタジーの世界で、クリスタルシャンデリアが輝き、落ち着いたクラシック音楽が流れ、制服を着たスタッフと、静かなフクロウたちが迎えてくれる。

　2014年にオープンして以来、親しみやすい雰囲気、鳥たちとたくさんふれあえ、静かでリラックスできる環境が、日本人にも観光客にも好評だ。

　ネットでの予約は簡単だ。日時が決まったら、予約の10分前に来店するよう言われる。制服を着たスタッフが鳥に接するときの一般的な注意事項以上の情報ファイル（日本語と英語）を手渡してくれる。フクロウの食性や、食事内容、瞳の色、動物に関する法律などの情報まで含まれている。鳥を扱うときの演技もすごい。オーナーのアナウンスに続き、スタッフが鳥の紐を引き、フクロウが止まり木に戻る様子を見せてくれる。まるでシートベルトの使用方法を説明する客室乗務員のようだ。

　ある常連の女性客はその日、どうしてもフクロウに会いたくなって、昼休みの時間に来たそうだ。フクロウたちの名前を全部知っていて、それぞれの性格も説明してくれた。はじめて来たという女性客は、自分の席で腕に乗せた小さなフクロウをうっとり見つめて静かな笑みを浮かべていた。きっとすぐにまた来店するだろう。

　20羽のフクロウたちは残らず人なつこく、さわられるのにも慣れている。

🕐 Data Box

Resident animals 店内にいる動物	owls	フクロウ
Station 最寄駅	Akihabara	秋葉原
Cover charge 基本料金	Entrance fee for a one-hour visit is 1,500 yen which includes a bottle of water and a souvenir photo. Reservation required	1時間滞在の入場料は1,500円（ペットボトルの水とおみやげの写真付　要予約）
Open hours 営業時間	11am-6pm weekdays, 11am-8pm weekends. Closed Tuesdays	平日　11:00～18:00　土日　11:00～20:00　火曜定休
Address 住所	Chiyoda-ku, Kanda Neribeicho 67 [3 minutes from Akihabara station (JR line); 5 minutes from Suehirocho station (Ginza line)]	千代田区神田練塀町67［秋葉原駅（JR線）から徒歩3分　末広町駅（銀座線）から徒歩5分］
Cafe menu カフェメニュー	bottled water only	ペットボトルの水のみ
Animal treats 動物のおやつ	none	なし

Website: http://akiba2960.com/　　　　　　　　　　Phone: unlisted

Forest of Owl
Akihabara

Although it just opened in May 2015, the cafe-bar Forest of Owl (Auru no Mori) is a game changer. Just pay the entrance fee and soft drink charge (a huge choice from a bank of vending machines), and you're set for an unlimited time with the birds. (Apparently there can be a time limit on weekends if it gets very busy, but weekdays you can nurse a drink there for hours.) Better still, no appointment is necessary.

As you'd expect from a venue that used to be a maid cafe in Akihabara, the decor is a little unusual. It's not exactly a forest of owls. Imagine a tropical-fish-loving, anime fan had opened a bar in the jungle and you'll get some idea of the atmosphere.

Owls are perched among verdant foliage in front of big screen TVs, aquarium tanks, champagne bottles and Christmas lights. The eclectic background music ranges from old-school jazz to Michael Bolton.

There are about a dozen birds to pet, photograph, and even perch on your hand or head. The species include barn owls, eagle-owls, scops and tawny owls. On our visit there were several hatchlings, and an impressive, hulking Eurasian eagle-owl who turned out to be just two months old.

The most popular bird is a northern white-faced owl, a cute and friendly little critter without a leash. He'll sit on your arm and pose for pictures before suddenly flying off to his perch, sending a staff member running to bring him back.

Overall: ☕☕☕☕☕☕☕
総合評価

Visitor amenities: ☕☕☕
店内設備

Animal interactivity: ☕☕☕☕
動物とのふれあい

アウルの森
秋葉原

2015年5月にオープンしたばかりのカフェ・バー〈アウルの森〉はこれまでにない斬新な店だ。入場料とソフトドリンクの料金（ずらりと並んだ自動販売機からいろいろ選べる）を支払えば、準備万端、あとは心ゆくまでフクロウたちとの時間を楽しめる。（ただし、土日の混雑時には時間制限がある場合がある。平日はワンドリンクで何時間もねばることができる）さらに、予約は一切不要だ。

以前はメイドカフェだったこともあり、店内の装飾はちょっと変わっている。厳密に言うと、ここはフクロウの森ではない。熱帯魚マニアのアニメファンがジャングルでバーを開いたような感じと言えば、少しは雰囲気が伝わるだろう。

大スクリーンのテレビ画面、水槽、シャンパンのボトル、クリスマスのような照明の前にあるフェイクグリーンで覆われた横木にフクロウたちは止まっている。BGMは本格的なジャズからマイケル・ボルトンまで幅広い。

20羽ほどの鳥がいて、さわったり、写真を撮ったり、手や頭に乗せたりもできる。メンフクロウ、ミミズク、コノハズク、モリフクロウなどがいる。私たちが訪れたときはヒナが何匹かいた。生後2か月になったばかりの大きなユーラシアンミミズクが目を引いた。

一番人気は、かわいくて人なつこく、紐でつながれていないアメリカオオコノハズクだ。腕に止まって、写真用にポーズをとってくれるが、途中で突然飛び立って止まり木に戻ってしまうので、スタッフが連れ戻すために追いかけることになる。

Data Box

Resident animals 店内にいる動物	owls	フクロウ
Station 最寄駅	Akihabara	秋葉原
Cover charge 基本料金	890 yen with soft drink, 1,080 yen with one beer, no time limit	ソフトドリンクプラン 890円 ビールプラン 1,080円 時間制限はなし
Open hours 営業時間	2pm-11pm; Wednesday 5pm-11pm	14:00〜23:00 水曜日は17:00〜23:00
Address 住所	Chiyoda-ku, Sotokanda 4-5-8 [3 minutes from Suehirocho station (Ginza line); 6 minutes from Akihabara station (JR line)]	東京都千代田区外神田4-5-8 [末広町駅（銀座線）から徒歩3分、秋葉原駅（JR線）から徒歩6分]
Cafe menu カフェメニュー	soft drinks 100 yen, beer 540 yen, bar snacks 200 yen	ソフトドリンク100円 ビール540円 おつまみ200円
Animal treats 動物のおやつ	none	なし

Website: http://2960.tokyo/ 　　　Phone: 03-3254-6366

Fuwafuwa
Yokohama

Billed as a "place you can meet owls," the Fuwafuwa cafe is a light, airy space just across the main road in front of Ichigao station. It's been open since April 2014, and offers a friendly parliament of twenty owls. Like the other hands-on venues in town, it's all about quality time with the owls—after a five-minute talk on bird-handling etiquette, you are free to pet the birds and take photos for the rest of the hour.

The busy but super-obliging manageress offers visitors the chance to pose with a bird on the hand, shoulder, or even head. One nice innovation is the full-length mirror that allows customers to photograph their reflections with the birds, who for some reason always look the other way at the crucial moment.

The owl selection features many familiar species available in other cafes, such as eagle-owl, rufous-legged owl, tropical screech owl, barn owl, sooty owl and tawny owl. They did have some species that we've not seen before in a cafe setting—including a bit-too-friendly spectacled owl and a tiny ferruginous pygmy owl that drew sighs of "Aww, so cute!" from the other guests.

On our visit, two birds were unavailable for photographs—like its famous fellow Hedwig from the Harry Potter movies, the imperious snowy owl was "resting" between roles in a corner, and Rou, the western screech owl, was on an extended nap because she was "a little old lady."

The fee includes a soft drink. Depending on the day, it may be possible to extend your visit by another thirty minutes. The shop can only take about a dozen visitors at one time, so it's best to make a reservation by phone.

Overall: ☕☕☕☕☕☕☕
総合評価

Visitor amenities: ☕☕☕
店内設備

Animal interactivity: ☕☕☕☕
動物とのふれあい

ふわふわ

横浜

「フクロウに会える店」〈ふわふわ〉は、市が尾駅前の大通りに面した、明るく広々とした店だ。オープンは2014年4月で、20羽の人なつこいフクロウたちがいる。さわってもよい他の店と同じく、なんといってもフクロウと過ごす時間を大切にしたい。フクロウの取りあつかいに関する説明を5分聞いたあとは、心ゆくまでなでたり、一緒に写真を撮ることができる。

オーナーの女性は忙しそうだが、サービス精神旺盛で、腕や肩、時には頭にまでフクロウを乗せてポーズをとらせてくれる。全身が映る鏡が置いてあるので、ここぞと言うときになぜか顔をそむけてしまうフクロウと写真を撮るときに便利だ。

ミミズク、アカアシモリフクロウ、スピックスコノハズク、メンフクロウ、ススイロメンフクロウ、モリフクロウなど他の店でもおなじみの品種がいる。しかし、カフェでは見たことのない種類もいた。少々馴れ馴れしいメガネフクロウと、他の客が「とってもかわいい！」と溜め息をもらしていた小さなアカスズメフクロウなどだ。

私たちの訪問時に、写真がとれなかったフクロウが2羽いる。映画「ハリー・ポッター」でおなじみのヘドウィグに似た、偉そうなシロフクロウは出番の合間で「休憩中」だったし、ロウという名前のニシアメリカオオコノハズクは、「おばあちゃんなので」長い昼寝の最中だった。

料金にはソフトドリンクが含まれている。日によっては30分延長も可能だ。一度に入店できるのは12人までなので、電話での予約がベストだ。

Data Box

Resident animals 店内にいる動物	owls	フクロウ
Station 最寄駅	Ichigao	市が尾
Cover charge 基本料金	1,500 yen for one hour. Reservation recommended	1時間1,500円　予約したほうがよい
Open hours 営業時間	2pm-8pm (Sat. Noon-8pm, Sun. 11am-6pm). Closed Thursdays	14:00～20:00（土曜12:00～20:00、日曜11:00～18:00）木曜定休
Address 住所	Yokohama-shi, Aoba-ku, Ichigaocho 1162-1 [2 minutes from Ichigao station (Denentoshi line)]	横浜市青葉市が尾町1162-1 ［市が尾駅（田園都市線）から徒歩2分］
Cafe menu カフェメニュー	soft drink included	ソフトドリンクが料金に含まれている
Animal treats 動物のおやつ	none	なし

Website: http://ameblo.jp/fuwafuwafukurou/

Phone: 080-7990-2960

Fukuro no Mise

◎ Osaka Minami Morimachi

The friendly, outgoing staff go out of their way to make a visit to this pioneering owl cafe a fun experience for visitors. Even the ten-minute bird-safety lecture, conducted with the help of a cute owl puppet, was surprisingly entertaining and had the crowd laughing.

After the lecture (which includes snippets of English) and the delivery of soft drinks or beer, visitors can enjoy forty minutes of quality bird time. The staff make sure everyone gets a chance to handle and interact with two or three birds during this time.

There are different rules of engagement for the various sizes of birds—for example small birds can sit happily on top of your head for photo ops, while medium-size birds can sit on your shoulder and large birds can rest on your arm after you've put on a leather glove or gauntlet.

Usually around six or eight birds are on active duty during each session, while the others (there are 24 in all) are on break—you can take pictures and engage in staring contests, but no touching.

Reservations can only be made in person at the shop, and there might be some waiting time on weekends, although we had only a minimal wait when we arrived early on a Sunday afternoon. The sign outside the shop says 'Owl Family' in English and 'Fukuro no Mise' ('Shop of Owls') in Japanese.

Overall: ☕☕☕☕☕☕
総合評価

Visitor amenities: ☕☕☕
店内設備

Animal interactivity: ☕☕☕
動物とのふれあい

フクロウのみせ

大阪　南森町

　フクロウカフェの草分け的存在であるこの店では、気さくで熱心なスタッフが客を楽しませてくれる。たった10分間だが、フクロウの指人形を使って面白おかしく安全に関する説明をしてくれるので、聞いていた人たちは爆笑していた。
　英語も少しまじえての説明が終わると、ソフトドリンクかビールが運ばれてきて、40分間フクロウと楽しい時間を過ごすことができる。この時間内に全ての客が2、3羽のフクロウを体に乗せたり、ふれあったりできるよう、スタッフが気を配っている。
　大きさによって、フクロウとのふれあいかたは異なる。例えば、小さいものなら写真を撮るときに、頭の上に乗せることができるが、中くらいのものは肩の上に乗せるし、大きなものは革製の手袋やコテをつけた上で腕に乗せることになっている。
　通常、各セッションでは6〜8羽のフクロウが店に出ていて、他は休憩している（全部で24羽いる）。写真撮影やにらめっこはできるが、勝手にさわることはできない。
　予約は直接店頭で。週末は待ち時間があるかもしれないが、私たちが日曜の午後早い時間に訪れたときは少し待つだけですんだ。店の外の看板には英語で"Owl Family"、日本語で「フクロウのみせ」とある。

🕐 Data Box

Resident animals 店内にいる動物	owls	フクロウ
Station 最寄駅	Minami Morimachi	南森町
Cover charge 基本料金	1,500 yen for one hour with soft drink, 1,700 yen for one hour with alcoholic beverage	1時間ソフトドリンク付き1,500円　1時間アルコール飲料付き1,700円
Open hours 営業時間	Noon-8pm Tuesday to Friday; 11am-8pm weekends and holidays. Closed Mondays	火曜〜金曜12:00〜20:00　土日祝日11:00〜20:00　月曜定休
Address 住所	Osaka-shi, Kita-ku, Tenjinbashi 1-10-13 [7 minutes from Minami Morimachi station (Tanimachi line) 7 minutes from Osaka Tenmangu station (JR line)]	大阪市北区天神橋1-10-13［南森町駅（谷町線、堺筋線）、大阪天満宮駅（JR線）から徒歩7分］
Cafe menu カフェメニュー	soft drinks and alcoholic beverages	各種ソフトドリンク、アルコール飲料
Animal treats 動物のおやつ	none	なし

Website: http://owlfamily.co.jp/　　　Phone: 06-6360-6205

Ikefukurou Cafe

Ikebukuro

Located just a few minutes south of Ikebukuro Station, the delightfully named Ikefukurou has fourteen owls for your viewing, photographing and petting pleasure. The place runs like clockwork as visitors are called in by name, given a short safety talk, and then allowed to spend the rest of the hour with the owls.

Choose from a fruit juice or beer for refreshment, and ask the staff to help you pose for photos with an owl on your hand or head. The friendly owls include an American eagle-owl, mottled owl, tawny owl, vermiculated eagle-owls, several species of scops owl and a tropical screech owl.

It's best to make a reservation the day before via email. The cover charge can be discounted by following the cafe on Facebook, Twitter and Instagram to a maximum of 300 yen.

Overall: ☕☕☕☕☕☕☕☕
総合評価

Visitor amenities: ☕☕☕
店内設備

Animal interactivity: ☕☕☕☕
動物とのふれあい

いけフクロウカフェ
池袋

池袋駅から南に数分歩いたところにある、ユニークな名前の〈いけフクロウ〉では、14匹のフクロウたちを眺めたり、撮影したりできる。店は規則正しく運営されている。客は名前で呼ばれると、安全に関する短い説明を聞き、それから残りの時間をフクロウたちと過ごすことを許される。

飲み物はフルーツジュースかビールを選べる。それから、スタッフにお願いして腕か頭にフクロウを乗せて写真を撮るのを手伝ってもらえる。アメリカワシミミズク、ナンベイヒナフクロウ、モリフクロウ、アビシニアンワシミミズク、何種類かのコノハズク、スピックスコノハズクなどの人なつこいフクロウたちがいる。

前日にメールで予約しておくとよい。フェイスブック、ツイッター、インスタグラムで店のアカウントをフォローすると、最大300円の割引がある。

Data Box

Resident animals 店内にいる動物	owls	フクロウ
Station 最寄駅	Ikebukuro	池袋
Cover charge 基本料金	1,400 yen for one hour, 1,600 yen for one hour on weekends and holidays, includes one drink	1時間1,400円　土日祝日は1時間1,600円　ワンドリンク付き
Open hours 営業時間	1pm-5pm, 6pm-8pm; Noon-7pm on weekends and holidays	13:00〜17:00、18:00〜20:00　土日祝日は12:00〜19:00
Address 住所	Toshima-ku, Minami-Ikebukuro 1-17-1, 6F [3 minutes from Ikebukuro station (JR line)]	豊島区南池袋1-17-1 崎本ビル6F [池袋駅（JR線、東武線、有楽町線など）から徒歩3分]
Cafe menu カフェメニュー	fruit juice or beer	フルーツジュースかビールのみ
Animal treats 動物のおやつ	none	なし

Website: http://www.ikefukuroucafe.com/

Phone: 03-5904-8344

Cafe Baron
Koenji

Baron is a very laid-back cafe where you can hang out with stunning resident owls and capricious lizards while you enjoy very good coffee, tea and snacks. There's a hands-off policy here—no touching the owls—but you can take all the photos you like as long as you respect each bird's personal space (and turn off your flash).

The enthusiastic proprietor clearly loves his birds, and he seems happy to spend the whole afternoon talking owl lore with his customers (mostly in Japanese). A small library of owl books is also available for perusal. A total of four birds are currently in residence—two great greys, a Ural owl and a barn owl—plus a yellow-headed water monitor and a mangrove monitor who can be seen cavorting in the lizard tanks.

Four or five small tables are lined up on one side of the cafe, with owl-themed artwork on the walls and knick-knacks (mostly for sale) on the shelves. The cafe is known for their Japanese curries, but they seem to run out by mid-afternoon so we ordered the hot apple tart instead, which turned out to be very good.

Dessert with an excellent coffee runs 700 yen, while curries start at around 1,000 yen; there's no cover charge. As a bonus for foreign visitors, the proprietor speaks fluent English.

Overall: ☕☕☕☕☕☕☕☕
総合評価

Visitor amenities: ☕☕☕☕☕
店内設備

Animal interactivity: ☕☕☕☕☕
動物とのふれあい

フクロウカフェ　Cafe Baron　高円寺

〈バロン〉はゆったりくつろげる場所だ。美しいフクロウと、気ままなトカゲがいて、おいしいコーヒー、お茶、軽食が楽しめる。動物にさわるのは禁止されているが、フクロウの邪魔にならないように（フラッシュはオフにしておくこと）、好きなだけ写真を撮ることができる。

店のフクロウを愛してやまないオーナーは、客相手にフクロウの話をしだすと、うれしそうにいつまでも話している（ほとんど日本語だ）。それほど量は多くないが、フクロウの本がそろっており、読むことができる。現在はカラフトフクロウが2羽、ウラルフクロウとメンフクロウが1羽ずつの計4羽のフクロウが店内にいる。他にはミズオオトカゲとマングローブオオトカゲが飼育ケースの中で動き回るのを観察できる。

小さなテーブルが4つか5つ片側に並んでいて、フクロウをモチーフにした手工芸品が壁に掛けられ、雑貨（多くは売り物）が棚に並べてある。カレーがおいしいと評判だが、午後遅い時間に入ったので売り切れだった。かわりにホットアップルタルトを注文したが、とてもおいしかった。

本格的なコーヒーとデザートのセットは700円、カレーは約1,000円からだ。基本料金はない。外国人観光客にはうれしいことに、オーナーは英語がペラペラだ。

Data Box

Resident animals 店内にいる動物	owls and lizards	フクロウ、トカゲ
Station 最寄駅	Koenji	高円寺
Cover charge 基本料金	None, but one drink or food order required	なし　ただし、ドリンクか料理の注文が必要
Open hours 営業時間	11am-6pm. Closed Wednesdays	11:00～18:00　水曜定休
Address 住所	Suginami-ku, Koenji-Kita 3-10-5 [6 minutes from Koenji station (JR line)]	杉並区高円寺北 3-10-5 [高円寺駅（JR線）から徒歩6分]
Cafe menu カフェメニュー	Coffee, curry and cake	コーヒー、カレー、ケーキ
Animal treats 動物のおやつ	None	なし

Website: http://fukuroucafe.blog.fc2.com/　　　Phone: 03-5356-6510

And a few more animals....

Cafe Little Zoo

Chiba

Located deep in suburban Chiba, Little Zoo has the feel of a neighborhood hangout frequented by a crowd of regulars. The cafe occupies an ordinary house, and has a resident animal population of three hawks and falcons (who live in the front yard), more than half a dozen owls (both indoors and outdoors), and various snakes, lizards, frogs and turtles that mostly stay in their tanks.

Many of the customers here are bird lovers, and some even bring their own owls to play with the resident birds. (Please consult with the staff before bringing your own bird.) You can drop in for coffee and cake, beers or wine in the evening, or a casual meal—their Thai-style green curry (1,000 yen with rice and salad) is tasty and quite spicy.

The avian talent includes eagle-owls, barn, tawny and little owls, Eurasian hobby, mountain hawk-eagle and northern goshawk. The reptiles include rarities such as the matamata turtle, pygmy spiny-tailed skink, armadillo girdled lizard, corn snake and the shy Nama padloper tortoise.

If you ask nicely, the staff will let you pet some of the owls. (Note that the staff don't speak English, so brush up on your owl- and reptile-related vocabulary if you need to.)

カフェ　リトルズー

千葉

　千葉県の郊外にある〈リトルズー〉は、たくさんいる常連客がリピートする地元の気軽な店といった雰囲気だ。民家風の店舗には、3羽の鷹とハヤブサが庭に、10羽近いフクロウが室内と屋外に、さまざまな種類のヘビ、トカゲ、カエル、カメが水槽の中にいる。

　客の大半は鳥好きで、ペットのフクロウを店で遊ばせるために連れてくる人もいる。(自分の鳥を連れてくるときは事前にスタッフに相談すること) コーヒーやケーキ、夕方にはビールやワイン、軽い食事も楽しめる。ここのグリーンカレー (ライスとサラダが付いて1,000円) はとても辛くておいしい。

　ミミズク、メンフクロウ、モリフクロウ、小型のフクロウ、チゴハヤブサ、クマタカ、オオタカなどの鳥類がいる。は虫類はマタマタ、デプレッサイワトカゲ、アルマジロトカゲ、コーンスネーク、恥ずかしがり屋のナマクアヒラセリクガメなど、珍しい種類がそろっている。

　うまくスタッフにお願いすれば、何羽かフクロウをさわらせてもらえるだろう。(スタッフは英語を話さないので、必要があればフクロウとは虫類関連の語彙をブラッシュアップしておくこと)

Overall: ☕☕☕☕☕
総合評価

Visitor amenities: ☕☕☕☕
店内設備

Animal interactivity: ☕☕
動物とのふれあい

 Data Box

Resident animals 店内にいる動物	hawks, owls, reptiles and amphibians	鷹、フクロウ、は虫類、両生類
Station 最寄駅	Keisei-Okubo	京成大久保
Cover charge 基本料金	None, but one drink or food order required	なし ただし、ドリンクか料理の注文が必要
Open hours 営業時間	Noon-8pm, noon-10pm on Friday/Saturday and the day before holidays. Closed Wednesday/Thursday	12:00〜20:00 金土祝日前日は12:00〜22:00 水曜・木曜定休
Address 住所	Chiba Prefecture, Narashino-shi, Moto-Okubo 1-4-10 [7 minutes from Keisei-Okubo station (Keisei main line)]	千葉県習志野市本大久保1-4-10 ［京成大久保駅（京成電鉄本線）から徒歩7分］
Cafe menu カフェメニュー	Full cafe menu with curry lunch sets, cake sets, coffee, beer, wine, etc.	カレーランチセット、ケーキセット、コーヒー、ビール、ワインなどメニューは豊富
Animal treats 動物のおやつ	none	なし

Website: http://little-zoo.jp/   Phone: 047-455-3329

インコ・オウム etc.

Tropical birds

Tori no Iru Cafe
Asakusa

The emphasis is on hands-on interaction with dozens of lively birds at this branch of the Tori no Iru Cafe. Located in a basement in touristy Asakusa, the cafe offers two very different experiences: a quiet moment with ten sleepy owls, and absolute bedlam with a flock of noisy, boisterous parrots and parakeets.

At the door, you're handed a rule sheet in English and Japanese, asked to disinfect your hands, and advised to don a protective poncho before entering the parrot area. You'll also be warned to open the door to the parrot room very gently, and to walk in carefully so as not to step on any birds that might be on the floor.

We recommend that you watch the clock because it's so much raucous fun in the parrot room that people can easily forget the time and incur extension fees (300 yen per fifteen minutes).

On our visit, the owls included two fledglings still in the process of molting their fluffy baby feathers. Along with the familiar Indian eagle-owl and scops owls, there was also a very rare milky eagle-owl with a price tag of one million yen. In the parrot room, a dozen vivid sun parakeets will flock to you, line up on your arms and head, and nibble on your ears and neck.

The lineup also includes rare birds such as a kookaburra, northern red-billed hornbill, white-throated toucan, and a crimson-and-blue female eclectus parrot, famous for its extreme sexual dimorphism—the male is emerald green. The loudness and friendliness of the shrieking, squawking parakeets can be a bit intense and overpowering for some, but most people find the hyperactive birds fascinating—hence the automatic time extensions.

There's a small shop selling owl- and bird-related goods at the entrance, and you can also purchase drinks.

Overall: ☕☕☕☕☕☕☕
総合評価

Visitor amenities: ☕☕☕
店内設備

Animal interactivity: ☕☕☕☕☕
動物とのふれあい

鳥のいるカフェ

浅草

浅草店では、たくさんいる元気な鳥たちとのふれあいを大切にしている。観光客が集まる浅草の地下にあるこの店では、2種類の体験ができる。眠っているように静かな10羽のフクロウたちとの落ち着いたひとときと、そうぞうしくて威勢のよいオウムやインコたちとのにぎやかな時間だ。

鳥部屋に入る前に、受付で英語と日本語でルールを書いた紙を渡され、手を消毒するよう言われる。ポンチョの着用もすすめられる。床に鳥がいるかもしれないので、鳥部屋のドアは静かに開けて、そっと入室するよう指示がある。

時計をしっかり見ておいたほうがいい。とてもにぎやかで楽しいので、つい時間を忘れ、追加料金が発生するかもしれない（15分ごとに300円）。

私たちが訪れたときは、ふわふわの産毛から生え変わりかけている子どものフクロウが2羽いた。おなじみのベンガルワシミミズクやコノハズクにまじって、100万円の値札がついた、希少なミルキーワシミミズクがいた。鳥部屋ではたくさんの色鮮やかなコガネメキシコインコが群がってきて、腕や頭に止まり、耳や首をつついてくるだろう。

入り口にはフクロウや鳥関連のグッズを販売する小さい店があり、飲み物も買えるようになっている。

Data Box

Resident animals 店内にいる動物	owls and tropical birds	フクロウ、熱帯の鳥
Station 最寄駅	Asakusa	浅草
Cover charge 基本料金	1,000 yen for 30 minutes, 1,500 yen for one hour	30分1,000円　1時間1,500円
Open hours 営業時間	1pm-8pm; 11am-8pm on weekends and holidays	13:00〜20:00　土日祝日 11:00〜20:00
Address 住所	Taito-ku, Asakusa 1-12-8, Oyama Bldg B1F [5 minutes from Asakusa station (Asakusa and Ginza lines)]	台東区浅草1-12-8　大山ビル地下1F　[浅草駅(浅草線・銀座線)から徒歩5分]
Cafe menu カフェメニュー	soft drinks	各種ソフトドリンク
Animal treats 動物のおやつ	none	なし

Website: http://toricafe.co.jp/asakusa/　　Phone: 03-6802-8572

Kotori no Ouchi Inko Cafe
Fujisawa-shi

Things can get pretty squawky in the bird room here, as parakeets, cockatiels and Java sparrows fly noisily overhead and the resident parrots keep a sharp eye on visitors, on the lookout for any sunflower seeds that might be in their possession.

Once you wash your hands and venture past the bird room's mesh curtain it's very much a hands-on experience—birds will happily perch on extended fingers as well as arms, shoulders and heads. Some of them enjoyed taking exploratory nibbles at fingernails, arms and camera straps to test for edibility.

While most of the birds were relatively gentle, we were a bit surprised by the lack of protective gloves, given the high level of interactivity. Let's just say that this is the first bird cafe we've been to where we felt like maybe we ought to have a safe word. At the very least, you'll want to wear long sleeves when you visit.

The one-hour cover charge includes one drink, and the proprietress handed us a small finch to play with while we sipped our iced tea in the cafe area. Perhaps the most unexpected sight was a tiny, one-month-old kitten, enthusiastically playing with a cat toy in the front of the shop and seemingly oblivious to the raucous avian activity going on all around.

The colorful species include sun parakeet, Pacific parrotlet, canary-winged parakeet, cockatiel, monk parakeet, sulphur-crested cockatoo and blue-and-yellow macaw.

(The shop—"House of Birds Parakeet Cafe" is a rough translation of the name—is located deep in suburban Kanagawa Prefecture, at a small station on the way to Fujisawa and Enoshima. Note that the staff speak only Japanese, as do the parrots.)

Overall: ☕☕☕☕☕☕
総合評価

Visitor amenities: ☕☕
店内設備

Animal interactivity: ☕☕☕☕☕
動物とのふれあい

ことりのおうち　インコカフェ　　藤沢市

　ここの鳥部屋はそうぞうしい。インコ、オカメインコ、文鳥がけたたましく頭の上を飛んでいくし、オウムは客に目を光らせている。ひまわりの種が奪えないか見張っているのだ。

　手を洗い、鳥部屋の仕切りのメッシュ素材のカーテンを開けてしまえば、あとは体験あるのみ。伸ばした手や、腕、肩、頭にも鳥たちがうれしそうに止まってくる。食べられるかどうか確かめるために、指の爪や腕やカメラのストラップをかじってみる鳥もいる。

　ほとんどが比較的おとなしい鳥ばかりとはいえ、これだけじかに接触するのに保護用の手袋がないのには少々驚いた。おそらく、これまでに訪れた鳥カフェのなかでも、ここは安全だから大丈夫と思わせてくれるはじめての店なのだ、ということにしておこう。長袖を着ていたほうが無難だ。

　１時間の基本料金にはドリンクも含まれている。私たちがカフェコーナーでアイスティーを飲んでいると、オーナーの女性が小鳥を手渡してくれた。生後１か月の子猫が店の入り口にいたのだが、まわりで騒がしくしている鳥たちなどには目もくれず、夢中になって猫用おもちゃで遊んでいたのは意外な光景だった。

　コガネメキシコインコ、マメルリハ、ソデジロインコ、オカメインコ、キバタン、ルリコンゴウインコなど色とりどりの種類がいる。

　("House of Birds Parakeet Cafe" は店名を大雑把に翻訳したものだ。神奈川県の郊外、藤沢から江ノ島へ向かう間の小さな駅の近くにある。スタッフもオウムも日本語しかしゃべらない)

🕐 Data Box

Resident animals 店内にいる動物	tropical birds	熱帯の鳥
Station 最寄駅	Chogo	長後
Cover charge 基本料金	1,200 yen for one hour including drink	1時間1,200円　ワンドリンク付き
Open hours 営業時間	11am-6pm	11:00 ~ 18:00
Address 住所	Kanagawa-ken, Fujisawa-shi, Takakura 641-5 [1 minute from Chogo station (Odakyu Enoshima line)]	神奈川県藤沢市高倉641-5 [長後駅（小田急江ノ島線）から徒歩1分]
Cafe menu カフェメニュー	soft drinks	各種ソフトドリンク
Animal treats 動物のおやつ	the staff may give you a few sunflower seeds to dispense	スタッフがひまわりの種をくれることがある

Website: https://www.facebook.com/kotori.aqua　　**Phone:** 080-3428-8792

Kotori Cafe
Omotesando

This unusual cafe is populated by a diverse flock of parrots, parakeets and cockatoos for your bird-watching enjoyment. If you're especially adventurous and want to make friends with a bird or two, after you've finished your coffee or tea you can spend five minutes in the interactive zone at the back of the cafe.

There, a staff member will explain the shop's rules, apply disinfectant to your hands, and show you (in Japanese) how to handle and gently play with the resident birds without getting bitten. On the afternoon of a recent visit the shop's cockatoo was in a very squawky mood, but the baby parrots were much more calm and playful.

While you're at the cafe you can enjoy some excellent tarts and cakes (from 800 yen) and a robust Kona coffee (800 yen), and inspect the bird-themed paraphernalia for sale in the shop area. Note that there's a one-hour time limit at the cafe, and a 500-yen charge for your five-minute hands-on session with the birds.

The aviary zone contains budgerigars, cockatiels, rosy-faced lovebirds, canary-barred parakeets and a red-rumped parrot. The petting zone in the back features a white-crested cockatoo, rosy-faced lovebird and Java sparrows.

Overall: ☕☕☕☕☕
総合評価

Visitor amenities: ☕☕☕
店内設備

Animal interactivity: ☕☕☕
動物とのふれあい

ことりカフェ
表参道

オウムや、インコ、キバタンなどいろいろな鳥の群れを見て楽しむことができる、他にはあまりない店だ。勇気があって、特定の鳥と仲良くなりたくなったら、コーヒーかお茶を飲んだあと、カフェの奥にあるふれあいスペースで5分間過ごすことができる。

ふれあいスペースでは、まずスタッフから店のルールの説明があり、手を消毒したあとは、どうやったら鳥に噛まれないで触れて、そっと遊ぶことができるか（日本語で）教えてくれる。私たちが行ったのは午後だった。キバタンはやかましかったが、オウムのヒナたちはとてもおとなしくて、一緒に遊べた。

カフェでは、本格的なタルトやケーキ（800円から）、あら挽きコナコーヒー（800円）を楽しめる。鳥をモチーフにした雑貨が店内で販売されているので、じっくり見ることができる。カフェには1時間の時間制限があり、鳥とのふれあい体験には500円かかる。

鳥のゾーンにはセキセイインコ、オカメインコ、コザクラインコ、サザナミインコ、ビセイインコなどがいる。奥のふれあいゾーンにはタイハクオウム、コザクラインコが1羽ずつと、文鳥が何羽かいる。

🕐 Data Box

Resident animals 店内にいる動物	tropical birds	熱帯の鳥
Station 最寄駅	Omotesando	表参道
Cover charge 基本料金	800 yen with one drink in the cafe, 500 yen for five minutes in the bird room	カフェでワンドリンク800円 鳥の部屋に入室 5分で500円
Open hours 営業時間	11am-7pm. Closed every third Monday	11:00〜19:00 定休日 第3月曜日
Address 住所	Minato-ku, Minami Aoyama 6-3-7 [7 minutes from Omotesando station (Ginza, Hanzomon and Chiyoda lines)]	港区南青山6-3-7［表参道駅（銀座線、半蔵門線、千代田線）から徒歩7分］
Cafe menu カフェメニュー	coffee, tea, soft drinks and cakes	コーヒー、お茶、ソフトドリンク、ケーキ
Animal treats 動物のおやつ	none	なし

Website: http://kotoricafe.jp/

Phone: 03-6427-5115

Kotori Cafe Kichijoji
Kichijoji

Some two dozen finches, parakeets and other small birds are on display at this second, smaller branch of Omotesando's Kotori Cafe, located right across the street from the Ghibli Museum. The birds occupy a couple of glassed-in areas looking out onto the cafe, and provide a lively backdrop for a post-Ghibli coffee break.

The birds are mostly colorful cockatiels, rosy-faced lovebirds and canary-barred parakeets. Unlike its sister branch, this cafe offers no opportunities to pet the birds in the aviary.

A coffee and cake set runs 1,620 yen, and the wide-ranging shop area sells everything from bird-themed calendars and coffee mugs to parrot plush toys.

Overall: ☕☕☕☕
総合評価

Visitor amenities: ☕☕☕
店内設備

Animal interactivity: ☕
動物とのふれあい

ことりカフェ 吉祥寺 吉祥寺

三鷹の森ジブリ美術館の道路を挟んだ向かい側にある小さなこの店は、表参道のことりカフェの2号店だ。40羽あまりの小鳥、インコなどの鳥たちが見られる。2か所ほどある鳥たちのエリアはガラス張りになっていて、カフェから眺めることができる。ジブリ美術館のあとのコーヒーブレイクにはうってつけの場所だ。

色とりどりのオカメインコ、コザクラインコ、サザナミインコなどがいる。姉妹店とは違い、鳥ルーム内で鳥にさわれるサービスはない。

ケーキセットは1,620円だ。ショップでは鳥のカレンダーや、マグカップ、オウムのぬいぐるみなど、さまざまなグッズを売っている。

Data Box

Resident animals 店内にいる動物	tropical birds	熱帯の鳥
Station 最寄駅	Kichijoji	吉祥寺
Cover charge 基本料金	800 yen with one drink	800円 ワンドリンク付き
Open hours 営業時間	10:30am-6pm. Closed every third Tuesday	10:30～18:00 定休日 第3火曜日
Address 住所	Mitaka-shi, Shimorenjaku 1-14-7 [14 minutes from Kichijoji station (JR and Inokashira lines)]	三鷹市下連雀1-14-7 [吉祥寺駅(JR線、井の頭線)から徒歩14分]
Cafe menu カフェメニュー	coffee, tea, soft drinks and cakes	コーヒー、お茶、ソフトドリンク、ケーキ
Animal treats 動物のおやつ	none	なし

Website: http://kotoricafe.jp/

Phone: 0422-29-9224

And a few more animals....

Yokohama Subtropical Teahouse Reptile Cafe

Yokohama Kannai

Lizards, tortoises, snakes and other reptiles—plus the odd amphibian—are the main attraction at this charming animal cafe. While most of the animals are confined to tanks or cages, several giant tortoises cavort around a large play area, where you can join them if it's before 5pm. There are also a couple of tame lizards that you can pet.

There's no cover charge per se, but you're expected to order a beverage or food. We tried the shop's "meat cakes," which turned out to be scones filled with Chinese-style BBQ pork (like what you'd get in a pork bun), and served with whipped cream. Beverages include more than a dozen varieties of tea—mostly Chinese. A pot of tea runs around 800–900 yen, while a plate of three scones (either meat, vegetable or fruit) plus tea is 1,400 yen.

The usual animal-cafe rules apply here—be gentle with the animals, sanitize your hands, and turn off the flash on your camera. Note that weekdays tend to be much less crowded than weekends.

The reptilian species here include an African spurred tortoise, spur-thighed tortoise, lined and leopard geckos, rainbow boa, corn snake, northern caiman lizard, green iguana and many others.

横浜亜熱帯茶館

横浜　関内

　この魅惑的な動物カフェの人気者はトカゲ、リクガメ、ヘビなどのは虫類に加え、両生類が一種類だけいる（ヤシヤモリ）。ほとんどは水槽やケージの中にいるが、大きなリクガメが何匹か広いプレイエリア内をのっしのっしと歩いていて、午後5時までならエリア内で一緒に歩くことができる。おとなしいトカゲも2、3匹さわることができる。

　基本料金はないが、飲み物か食べ物の注文が必要だ。私たちは「肉の惣菜ケーキ」を注文してみたのだが、中華風の豚肉炒め（肉まんの中に入っているようなもの）が包んであるスコーンがホイップクリームと一緒に出てきた。飲み物は10種類以上のお茶があるが、ほとんど中国茶だ。お茶は1ポット800～900円で、惣菜ケーキ3つ（肉、野菜、果物）とお茶のセットは1,400円だ。

　一般的な動物カフェと注意することは同じだ。動物にはやさしくしよう。必ず手の消毒をすること。カメラのフラッシュはオフにしておこう。土日に比べ、平日はかなりすいている。

　ケヅメリクガメ、ギリシャリクガメ、ヤシヤモリ、ヒョウモントカゲモドキ、レインボーボア、コーンスネーク、ギアナカイマントカゲ、グリーンイグアナなど、多くのは虫類がいる。

Overall: 🍵🍵🍵🍵🍵
総合評価

Visitor amenities: 🍵🍵🍵🍵
店内設備

Animal interactivity: 🍵🍵
動物とのふれあい

 Data Box

Resident animals 店内にいる動物	reptiles and amphibians	は虫類、両生類
Station 最寄駅	Kannai	関内
Cover charge 基本料金	One drink and food order required	ワンドリンクと食べ物の注文が必要
Open hours 営業時間	11am-7pm. Closed Tuesdays, Wednesdays	11:00〜19:00 火曜、水曜定休
Address 住所	Yokohama-shi, Naka-ku, Chojamachi 8-133 2F [7 minutes from Kannai station (JR line)]	横浜市中区長者町 8-133 冨森商事 2F ［関内駅（JR 線）から徒歩 7 分］
Cafe menu カフェメニュー	Chinese tea from 800 yen, snacks	中国茶 800 円から　軽食
Animal treats 動物のおやつ	none	なし

Website: http://www.reptilescafe.net/yokohama/heng_bang_ya_re_dai_cha_guan_Top.html
Phone: 045-263-4015

うさぎ

Rabbits

Mimi
Ikebukuro

Mimi has some of the friendliest and most relaxed rabbits we've encountered in Tokyo—we were impressed with how well they get along with each other, and how easy-going they are with human visitors. Unlike other cafes that allow only one or two rabbits out of their cages at one time, the playroom at Mimi is a non-stop rabbit party.

The one-hour cover charge here includes one drink, with some fifty varieties of coffee, tea and herbal tea to choose from. Also included is a small cup of rabbit kibble, which definitely helps to break the ice. After you've sanitized your hands and put on the apron that's provided, you can find a seat in the main playroom (or the smaller room if the cafe is crowded), and meet the eleven resident bunnies. The breeds include Jersey Wooly, Netherland Dwarf, Mini Rex, Poland Lop and others.

As usual, try to visit on a weekday if you can, to avoid the crowds. Reservations can be made by phone or email (check the website). Note that the front door is often locked, so give it a knock or call the phone number posted on the door if you don't get an answer.

Overall: ☕☕☕☕☕☕
総合評価

Visitor amenities: ☕☕☕☕◐
店内設備

Animal interactivity: ☕☕☕☕☕
動物とのふれあい

うさぎカフェ mimi 池袋

<mimi>のうさぎたちは、東京で出会ったどのうさぎよりも人なつこくリラックスしている。うさぎ同士仲がよく、人間の客にもフレンドリーなので感動した。他の店のように一度に1、2匹のうさぎしか外に出さないということもなく、ここのプレイルームは常にうさぎたちでいっぱいだ。

1時間の基本料金にはワンドリンクが含まれているが、コーヒー、お茶、ハーブティーなど50あまりのチョイスのなかから選べる。うさぎ用おやつもワンカップ無料で、仲良くなるのに役立つだろう。手の消毒をして、渡されたエプロンを着て、メインプレイルームに席を確保すれば(店内混雑時は小部屋に案内される)、11匹のうさぎたちとのご対面だ。ジャージーウーリー、ネザーランドドワーフ、ミニレッキス、ホーランドロップなどの品種がいる。

ここでも、すいている平日の来店がおすすめだ。予約は電話かEメールで(ホームページを参照のこと)入り口のドアは鍵がかかっていることが多いので、応答がなければ、ノックするか、ドアに書いてある電話番号にかけてみよう。

Data Box

Resident animals 店内にいる動物	rabbits	うさぎ
Station 最寄駅	Ikebukuro	池袋
Cover charge 基本料金	800 yen for 30 minutes; 1,200 yen for one hour with drink (1,300 yen on weekends)	30分800円 1時間ドリンク付きで1,200円 (土日は1,300円)
Open hours 営業時間	Noon-9pm (last admission 8pm); 10am-9pm (last admission 8pm) on weekends and holidays	12:00～21:00 (最終入場20:00)、土日祝日は10:00～21:00 (最終入場20:00)
Address 住所	Toshima-ku, Higashi Ikebukuro 1-13-9 Karasukoma #2 Bldg. 8F [5 minutes from Ikebukuro station East Exit (JR line)]	豊島区東池袋1-13-9 烏駒第2ビル8F [池袋駅(JR線、東武線、有楽町線など)東口から徒歩5分]
Cafe menu カフェメニュー	56 varieties of coffee and tea	56種類ものコーヒーと紅茶
Animal treats 動物のおやつ	complimentary rabbit kibble	無料のうさぎ用おやつ

Website: http://www.usa-mimi.com   Phone: 070-5079-3841

Usayu
Osaka Ibaraki City

Much more comfortable and spacious than other rabbit cafes we've been to, this charming suburban shop is spread out over three rooms and organized into nine separate rabbit play areas, so visitors can get to know the rabbits one at a time. We visited on a busy Sunday afternoon, but even then there were plenty of rabbits to go around, with opportunities to exchange rabbits whenever we liked.

The interior is filled with sundry stuffed animal toys, bunny slippers, and just about any kind of rabbit-themed ornament you can imagine, making for some cute photo ops. Most rabbit zones include raised platforms and a seating area big enough for a couple of visitors, along with a fenced-off section of floor. Aprons are provided to protect your clothing.

A rather outgoing English Angora rabbit was recommended by the staff, who characterized it as being not very rabbit-like. We also played with a massive grey French Angora rabbit named Rum (or possibly "Lamb"), who weighed in at 4kg. Luckily we took notes, because at the end of our visit we were quizzed on which were our favorite rabbits.

Coffee and other soft drinks are free of charge from the self-service machine, included in the cover charge. We were also provided with a small cup of rabbit chow at one point, although our chosen rabbit seemed just as interested in chomping on hay—perhaps he had had a big lunch.

Overall: ☕☕☕☕☕☕
総合評価

Visitor amenities: ☕☕☕☕
店内設備

Animal interactivity: ☕☕☕☕☕
動物とのふれあい

うさゆ

大阪　茨木市

他のうさぎカフェに比べ、ゆったり広々とした郊外型の感じのいい店だ。店内は3部屋あって、うさぎのプレイエリアは9つに分かれている。だから、一対一でうさぎと遊べるのだ。混んでいる日曜の午後に行ったのだが、その時間帯でもフリーのうさぎがいたし、自由にうさぎを取り換えることができた。

室内はさまざまなうさぎのぬいぐるみや、うさぎのスリッパなど、ありとあらゆるうさぎグッズであふれていて、かわいい写真が撮れる。うさぎエリアのそばには、フェンスで囲まれた場所に低いテーブルと、二人掛けのソファが置いてある。服が汚れないように、エプロンがもらえる。

店員が、この子はうさぎらしくないからと言って、元気のよいイングリッシュアンゴラをすすめてくれた。「ラム」という名前のとても大きなグレーのフレンチアンゴラとも遊んだが、4キロあるそうだ。帰るときにどのうさぎが一番よかったか聞かれたのだが、メモをとっていたから助かった。

コーヒーやソフトドリンク代は基本料金に含まれているので、無料でセルフサービスの機械からとることができる。途中で小さなカップに入ったうさぎのおやつをもらったのだが、私たちと遊んでいたうさぎは干し草ばかり食べていた。きっと食事のあとで満腹だったのだろう。

🕐 Data Box

Resident animals 店内にいる動物	rabbits	うさぎ
Station 最寄駅	Ibaraki	茨木
Cover charge 基本料金	1,300 for one hour with free drinks; 500 yen for each additional thirty minutes	1時間 1,300 円フリードリンク付き　延長は 30 分ごとに 500 円
Open hours 営業時間	1pm-7pm (last admission 6pm). Closed Wednesdays, Thursdays	13:00 〜 19:00（最終入場 18:00）水曜、木曜定休
Address 住所	Osaka-fu, Ibaraki-shi, Matsugamotocho 3-16, Bardens Club Bldg 2F [5 minutes from Ibaraki station (JR Tokaido line)]	大阪府茨木市松ケ本町 3-16 バーデンズクラブビル 2F ［JR 茨木駅（JR 東海道線）から徒歩 5 分］
Cafe menu カフェメニュー	coffee, tea and soft drinks	コーヒー、お茶、ソフトドリンク
Animal treats 動物のおやつ	small, complimentary cups of rabbit snacks	小さなカップに入ったうさぎフード

Website: http://www.usa-yu.com/　　　　Phone: 072-629-6661

Usagi Cafe Ohisama
Shimo-Kitazawa

More spacious than the average rabbit cafe, Ohisama is divided into a glassed-in play area, where you can feed and pet the bunnies, and a couple of different lounge areas where you can relax over a cup of coffee and peruse rabbit-related manga and other literature.

Inside the play area, one wall is lined with seats while the opposite wall is stacked with cages for some two dozen rabbits of various breeds and sizes. Generally only two or three rabbits are running around outside their cages at any given time. If you want to make friends more quickly, rabbit snacks consisting of dried vegetables are available for 100 yen.

Ohisama is unusual among animal cafes in that they serve full meals as well as drinks. For 2,300 yen, you can get a pasta dish, salad, small dessert and drink, plus ninety minutes of rabbit time. If you just want coffee or juice, the cover charge includes one drink.

Overall: ☕☕☕☕☕☕
総合評価

Visitor amenities: ☕☕☕☕
店内設備

Animal interactivity: ☕☕☕☕
動物とのふれあい

うさぎカフェ　おひさま　下北沢

　一般的なうさぎカフェよりも広々としている〈おひさま〉は、うさぎに食べ物を与えたり、なでたりできるガラス張りのプレイエリアと、コーヒーを飲んでくつろぎ、うさぎ関連のマンガや本を読むことができる2つのラウンジエリアに分かれている。

　プレイエリアでは、一方の壁側にソファが並べてあり、その向かいにはいろいろな種類、大きさの20匹あまりのうさぎたちの入ったケージがある。通常、ケージの外で遊んでいるうさぎは2、3匹だ。早く仲良くなりたいのなら、うさぎのおやつ（乾燥野菜）が100円で買える。

　飲み物だけでなく、しっかりした食事を出す〈おひさま〉のような動物カフェはあまりない。パスタ、サラダ、デザート、飲み物と90分間のうさぎタイムがついて2,300円だ。コーヒーやジュースだけでよいのなら、ワンドリンクが基本料金に含まれている。

🕐 Data Box

Resident animals 店内にいる動物	rabbits	うさぎ
Station 最寄駅	Shimo-Kitazawa	下北沢
Cover charge 基本料金	1,000 yen for 30 minutes with one drink, 1,400 yen for one hour with one drink	30分1,000円　1時間1,400円　ワンドリンク付き
Open hours 営業時間	Noon-8pm	12:00〜20:00
Address 住所	Setagaya-ku, Kitazawa 2-18-5 2F [3 minutes from Shimo-Kitazawa station South Exit (Odakyu and Inokashira lines)]	世田谷区北沢2-18-5 2F［下北沢駅（小田急線、井の頭線）南口から徒歩3分］
Cafe menu カフェメニュー	free coffee and soft drinks, desserts from 350 yen, meals from 700 yen	コーヒー、各種ソフトドリンクは無料　デザート350円から　食事は700円から
Animal treats 動物のおやつ	rabbit snacks 100 yen	うさぎ用スナック 100円

Website: http://www.rabicafe.com/　　Phone: 03-3410-5299

Floche
Yotsuya

Basically a rabbit pet shop and pet hotel, Floche has set up a tiny cafe area where you can enjoy a coffee break with rabbits in the background. If you want more interaction, there's a playroom area where you can feed and play with one rabbit at a time, and exchange rabbits whenever you like.

Our first rabbit, which resembled a fluffy grey mophead, was on the shy side, but the second one—a big brown English rabbit (so we were told) with long floppy ears was extremely sociable. And also quite demanding, as long as we had snacks in our possession. By the way the snack plate on offer here for 150 yen is one of the more deluxe versions in town, with shiso leaves and parsley adding some variety to the usual carrots and lettuce.

In addition to time in the playroom you can visit and feed the other rabbits in their cages. There were at least a couple dozen here, of all shapes and sizes, many of them very pretty. Most of the rabbits are for sale, so this is a good place to get to know your rabbit's personality before you adopt.

The cafe menu includes coffee, juice, ice cream and cake, and prices start at around 500 yen for iced coffee. There's a separate cover charge (600 yen) for time in the playroom.

Overall: ☕☕☕☕☕☕☕☕
総合評価

Visitor amenities: ☕☕☕☕☕
店内設備

Animal interactivity: ☕☕☕☕☕
動物とのふれあい

うさぎのお店 Floche

四谷

基本的にはペットショップ兼ペットホテルの〈フロッシュ〉には小さなカフェスペースがあり、うさぎを眺めながらコーヒーを楽しむことができる。もっとふれあいたかったら、プレイルームで一度に一匹のうさぎにエサをあげたり、遊んだりできる。うさぎを取り換えるのも自由だ。

私たちの最初のうさぎはモフモフの灰色モップみたいだったが、恥ずかしがり屋だった。次は、店の人によると「イングリッシュ・ラビット」の、長い耳を垂らした大きな茶色のうさぎで、とても人なつこかった。しかも、食べ物を持っているとしつこくせがまれた。ところで、150円で買えるおやつは他の店に比べて豪華で、よくあるニンジンとレタスの他に、シソの葉とパセリが入っている。

プレイルームでふれあう以外にも、ケージにいるうさぎにエサを与えることができる。常時20匹くらいの、さまざまな形や大きさのかわいいうさぎたちがいる。ほとんどが購入可能だ。ペットとして迎える前に、うさぎの性格を知るのによい場所だ。

Data Box

Resident animals 店内にいる動物	rabbits	うさぎ
Station 最寄駅	Yotsuya	四谷
Cover charge 基本料金	600 yen for 30-minute rental of a rabbit play booth, plus one order from the cafe menu	ふれあいブースでのうさぎレンタル 30分600円 カフェメニューからワンオーダー必要
Open hours 営業時間	Noon-7pm on weekends and holidays; Closed weekdays	土、日、祝日 12:00～19:00 平日定休
Address 住所	Shinjuku-ku, Yotsuya 1-22-12 KR Bldg. 2F [4 minutes from Yotsuya station (JR, Marunouchi and Namboku lines)]	東京都新宿区四谷1-22-12 KRビル2F〔四谷駅から徒歩4分（JR線、丸の内線、南北線）〕
Cafe menu カフェメニュー	soft drinks from 500 yen	各種ソフトドリンク 500円から
Animal treats 動物のおやつ	rabbit snack plate 150 yen	うさぎのおやつプレート 150円

Website: http://ameblo.jp/usagi-floche/   Phone: 03-5341-4248

Ra.a.g.f
Jiyugaoka

The larger of the two branches of this popular rabbit cafe, Ra.a.g.f Jiyugaoka has around two dozen rabbits of various breeds for visitors to play with and feed. Seating is on cushions on the floor, at tiny tables in two separate play areas.

The rabbits here come in a variety of sizes and colors, with one huge resident weighing in at 4.4 kilograms. Breeds include Holland Lop, French Lop, Netherland Dwarf, American Fuzzy Lop, Jersey Wooly, and Lionhead and Angora mixes.

Usually two to four rabbits are running around loose at any given time, and you can choose the rabbits you want to play with, although some might be "on a break" and therefore not available. A dish of greens and carrots for feeding the rabbits is 150 yen, while coffee and soft drinks are free.

Note that this location isn't quite as tourist-friendly as the Harajuku branch—staff instructions are usually all in Japanese, and there's a surprisingly detailed agreement (in Japanese) that visitors are asked to sign. Once you're past the paperwork though, this is one of the more laid-back animal cafes around town, especially on weekdays when they're less busy.

Overall: ☕☕☕☕☕☕☕☕☕☕
総合評価

Visitor amenities: ☕☕☕☕☕
店内設備

Animal interactivity: ☕☕☕☕☕
動物とのふれあい

Ra.a.g.f（ラフ） 自由が丘

人気のうさぎカフェ〈Ra.a.g.f〉の自由が丘店は規模が大きく、20匹あまりのさまざまな種類のうさぎたちと遊んでエサを与えることができる。2つあるプレイエリアには、それぞれ小さな座卓があって、座布団の上に座ることになる。

いろいろな大きさ、色のうさぎたちがいて、4.4キロもある巨大うさぎもいた。ホーランドロップ、フレンチロップ、ネザーランドドワーフ、アメリカンファジーロップ、ジャージーウーリー、ライオンヘッドとアンゴラの雑種などがいる。

常に2～4匹のうさぎがフロアで跳ね回っているし、遊びたいうさぎを選ぶことができるが、「休憩中」の場合は遊べない。うさぎのおやつは葉物野菜とニンジンで、150円。コーヒーとソフトドリンクは無料。

原宿店よりも外国人観光客慣れしていないようだ。スタッフの説明はすべて日本語で、とても細かい承諾書（日本語で書いてある）にサインを求められる。書類の記入を済ませば、混んでいない平日はとくに、都内の動物カフェのなかでもゆったり過ごせる部類に入る。

Data Box

Resident animals 店内にいる動物	rabbits	うさぎ
Station 最寄駅	Jiyugaoka	自由が丘
Cover charge 基本料金	700 yen for 30 minutes, 1,100 yen for one hour, 550 yen for each additional 30 minutes	30分700円　1時間1,100円　延長は30分550円
Open hours 営業時間	Noon-7:30pm (last admission 7pm); 11am-8pm (last admission 7:30pm) on weekends and holidays. Closed Thursdays	12:00～19:30（最終入場19:00）　土日祝日は11:00～20:00（最終入場19:30）木曜定休
Address 住所	Meguro-ku, Jiyugaoka 1-26-3 Jiyugaoka Masumoto Bldg. 5F [2 minutes from Jiyugaoka station (Tokyu Toyoko/Oimachi lines)]	目黒区自由が丘1-26-3 自由が丘升本ビル5F　[自由が丘駅（東急東横線、大井町線）から徒歩2分]
Cafe menu カフェメニュー	free coffee and soft drinks	コーヒーと各種ソフトドリンク無料
Animal treats 動物のおやつ	rabbit snacks 150 yen	うさぎ用スナック150円

Website: http://raagf.com/shop/jiyugaoka/   **Phone:** 03-3725-2240

Ra.a.g.f
Harajuku

Visitors are encouraged to pet, play with and feed the dozen or so rabbits "on staff" at this small backstreet cafe. Several different breeds are represented, and most of them seem to be quite lively (especially compared to typical residents of a cat cafe).

The cafe's interior space is relatively small—just three tiny tables, with floor seating for visitors. The rabbits take turns scampering about and spending time in their cages, with only a few running loose at any given time, although you can play with the ones in their cages too.

A dish of greens and shredded carrots for feeding the rabbits is 150 yen, and coffee and soft drinks are included in the cover charge.

There is a wide variety of breeds at this venue including Holland Lop, French Lop, Netherland Dwarf, American Fuzzy Lop, Jersey Wooly, and Lionhead and Angora mixes. If you're in the mood for a rabbit cafe tour of Tokyo, Ra.a.g.f also has a somewhat larger branch in Jiyugaoka, with around two dozen rabbits. The shop's initials stand for "rabbit and grow fat," in case you were wondering.

Overall: ☕☕☕☕☕☕☕
総合評価

Visitor amenities: ☕☕☕
店内設備

Animal interactivity: ☕☕☕☕☕
動物とのふれあい

Ra.a.g.f（ラフ）   原宿

　路地裏にある小さなこのカフェでは、10匹あまりいる「うさぎスタッフ」を存分になでたり、一緒に遊んだり、おやつを与えたりして楽しむことができる。数種類のうさぎたちがいて、（よくある猫カフェの猫たちとは違い）活発な子も多い。

　店内は広くはない。小さな座卓が3つ置いてあり、客はその周りに座ることになる。うさぎは交代で、フロアを走り回ったり、ケージで過ごしたりしている。常時フロアにいるのは2、3匹だが、ケージに入っているうさぎとも遊ぶことができる。

　うさぎのおやつの薄切りニンジンと葉物野菜は100円で買える。コーヒーやソフトドリンクは基本料金に含まれている。

　ホーランドロップ、フレンチロップ、ネザーランドドワーフ、アメリカンファジーロップ、ジャージーウーリー、ライオンヘッドとアンゴラの雑種など、たくさんの品種がいる。東京のうさぎカフェめぐりをしてみたいのなら、自由が丘に規模の大きな姉妹店があって、20匹ぐらいのうさぎがいる。店の名前が何を意味するのか気になる人もいるだろう。"Rabbit and grow fat"「うさぎと一緒に福来たる」だ。

Data Box

Resident animals 店内にいる動物	rabbits	うさぎ
Station 最寄駅	Harajuku	原宿
Cover charge 基本料金	700 yen for 30 minutes, 1,100 for one hour, 550 yen for each additional 30 minutes	30分 700円　1時間 1,100円　延長は30分 550円
Open hours 営業時間	Noon-7:30pm (last admission 7pm); 11am-8pm (last admission 7:30pm) on weekends and holidays. Closed Fridays	12:00〜19:30（最終入場19:00）　土日祝日は11:00〜20:00（最終入場19:30）金曜定休
Address 住所	Shibuya-ku, Jingumae 6-14-15, Maison Harajuku 3F [5 minutes from Meiji-Jingumae station Exit A7 (Chiyoda and Hanzomon lines); 8 minutes from Harajuku station (JR line)]	渋谷区神宮前6-14-15 メゾン原宿3F ［明治神宮前駅（千代田線、半蔵門線）A7出口から徒歩5分］
Cafe menu カフェメニュー	free coffee and soft drinks	コーヒーと各種ソフトドリンク無料
Animal treats 動物のおやつ	rabbit snacks 150 yen	うさぎ用スナック 150円

Website: http://raagf.com/shop/harajuku/　　Phone: 03-6805-0328

Usagi no Ehon
Shimo-Kitazawa

Even among Tokyo's animal cafes, Usagi no Ehon (Rabbit Picturebook) pushes the twee end of the scale, with dozens of children's picture books lining the walls, shelves filled with bunny-themed knick-knacks and plush toys, and a decor heavily influenced by late-period Peter Rabbit. It's the smaller of Shimo-Kitazawa's two rabbit cafes, and most seating is on the floor at miniature tables in a common play area, where a few rabbits at a time roam free.

There are also a couple of fenced-in pen areas that you can step into for more one-on-one rabbit time, and other rabbits you can visit in their cages. When you arrive you're issued a small dish of rabbit treats which you can dispense as you see fit. Around seven rabbits are on active duty, although not all are running around at any given time. The bunnies here are the very popular Holland Lop and Netherland Dwarf breeds, or hybrids.

In addition to the cover charge, you must also order food or a beverage from the menu. Drinks are 550 yen, while food items include pancakes and a pasta lunch of the day. We were lucky enough to snag the only normal-size table for our lunch—a very tasty spaghetti pepperoncino with bacon and spring vegetables. Our pasta plus iced coffee came to 950 yen.

Overall: ☕☕☕☕☕☕☕☕☕
総合評価

Visitor amenities: ☕☕☕☕☕
店内設備

Animal interactivity: ☕☕☕☕☕
動物とのふれあい

うさぎの絵本

下北沢

　数ある東京のアニマルカフェのなかでも、〈うさぎの絵本〉は独自のこだわりを持った店で、壁には子ども向け絵本がずらっと並び、棚にはうさぎの小物やぬいぐるみが所狭しと並んでいて、ピーターラビットの世界が広がっている。下北沢にあるうさぎカフェ2店のうち、小さいほうだ。プレイエリアではたいてい床の上に腰を下ろすことになり、うさぎが2、3匹あたりをうろついている。フェンスで仕切られているエリアも2つほどあり、中に入れば、一対一でのうさぎとのふれあいを楽しめるし、ケージの中のうさぎにも会える。入店すると、小さな皿にのったうさぎのおやつを渡され、好きなときに与えることができる。店内には7匹ほどのうさぎが待機しているが、外に出ているのは一部のうさぎだけだ。人気のホーランドロップ、ネザーランドドワーフと、雑種のうさぎがいる。

　基本料金に加え、食べ物か飲み物をメニューから注文しなくてはならない。飲み物は550円だ。食べ物はケーキ類と日替わりパスタがある。私たちは運よく普通サイズのテーブルに陣取ってランチを食べることができた。ベーコンと春野菜のペペロンチーノはとてもおいしかった。パスタとアイスコーヒーで950円だった。

🕐 Data Box

Resident animals 店内にいる動物	rabbits	うさぎ
Station 最寄駅	Shimo-Kitazawa	下北沢
Cover charge 基本料金	150 yen for 30 minutes plus one order from the set menu	30分150円　セットメニューからワンオーダーが必要
Open hours 営業時間	2pm-7pm; 1pm-6pm on weekends and holidays. Closed Mondays	14:00～19:00　土日祝日は 13:00～18:00　月曜定休
Address 住所	Setagaya-ku, Kitazawa 3-30-1 K Bldg. 2F [7 minutes from Shimo-Kitazawa station (Odakyu and Inokashira lines)]	世田谷区北沢3-30-1 Kビル2F [下北沢駅（小田急線、井の頭線）から徒歩7分]
Cafe menu カフェメニュー	set menu of cake or light meal and drink from 750 yen to 950 yen	ケーキ、もしくは軽食と飲み物のセットメニュー750円から950円
Animal treats 動物のおやつ	rabbit snacks	うさぎ用スナック

Website: http://usaginoehon.web.fc2.com/　　　Phone: 03-3466-5081

Candy Fruit Usagi no Yakata
Akihabara

Despite its location in the heart of Akihabara, the Candy Fruit Usagi no Yakata (Rabbit Mansion) isn't exactly a maid cafe—rather it's a rabbit cafe where the staff happen to be dressed in maid's uniforms. And perhaps it draws a higher ratio of male customers than other rabbit cafes. Other than that it shares typical rabbit-cafe characteristics—it has something of a pet-shop atmosphere, and the walls are lined with cages full of rabbits that you can pet and feed.

After you've placed your drink order, the staff will inquire as to which rabbit you want to spend some time with. On our visit, when we asked for a frisky rabbit, we were advised that a more docile bunny might be better for photographs. We were recommended Omochi, a female Holland Lop with droopy ears and double chin. There are twenty-one resident rabbits in total, with names and vital data marked on the front of each cage. Many of the rabbits are also available for sale should you decide to adopt a pet.

Seating is on floor cushions, either in the main space or in the two semi-enclosed booths. Generally there's a limit of one rabbit allowed to run around in each area of the cafe at any given time, but you can switch rabbits whenever you like. A 200-yen dish of vegetable snacks goes a long way in helping you make friends.

Coffee, tea, and other soft drinks are included in the entrance fee, but note there is a surcharge of 500 yen if you want to take photos with a camera (as opposed to a cellphone).

Overall: ☕☕☕☕☕☕☕☕
総合評価

Visitor amenities: ☕☕☕☕☕
店内設備

Animal interactivity: ☕☕☕☕☕
動物とのふれあい

キャンディフルーツ　うさぎの館 秋葉原

〈キャンディフルーツ　うさぎの館〉は秋葉原の中心にあるのだが、メイドカフェというよりは、スタッフがたまたまメイドの姿をしているうさぎカフェである。他のうさぎカフェより男性客の割合が高いようだ。その他は普通のうさぎカフェと変わらない。ペットショップのような雰囲気もあって、壁にずらりと並んだうさぎのケージの中には、うさぎがたくさんいて、さわったり、エサを与えることができる。

飲み物を注文したあとで、どのうさぎと過ごしたいか、スタッフから聞かれる。よく動くうさぎを希望したのだが、写真を撮るにはもっとおとなしいうさぎのほうがよいとアドバイスを受けた。「おもち」という名前の、耳が垂れて二重あごのホーランドロップをすすめられた。店内には全部で21匹のうさぎがいて、名前や生体情報は、それぞれのケージに表示してある。ペットとして飼うつもりなら、大半のうさぎは購入可能だ。

メインスペースか、ゆるやかに仕切られた半個室で床に置いてあるクッションに腰を下ろすことになる。店内のそれぞれのエリアで、ケージから出してよいうさぎは一度に一匹までという制限があるが、うさぎを取り換えるのは自由だ。200円で野菜のおやつが一皿買える。うさぎと仲良くなるのに役立つだろう。

入場料金にはコーヒー、お茶、ソフトドリンクの代金が含まれているが、カメラで撮影する場合は追加料金が500円かかるので注意が必要だ（携帯カメラ等での撮影は無料）。

Data Box

Resident animals 店内にいる動物	rabbits	うさぎ
Station 最寄駅	Akihabara	秋葉原
Cover charge 基本料金	1,100 yen (1,300 on weekends) for 30 minutes, 1,800 yen for one hour, includes soft drinks	30分 1,100円（土日は1,300円）、1時間 1,800円　ソフトドリンク付き
Open hours 営業時間	2pm-9:30pm; Noon-9:30pm weekends and holidays	14:00〜21:30　土日祝日は12:00〜21:30
Address 住所	Chiyoda-ku, Soto-Kanda 4-6-2, Isuzu Bldg 9F [2 minutes from Suehirocho station Exit 1 (Ginza line)]	東京都千代田区外神田4-6-2 いすゞビル9F [末広町（銀座線）1番出口から徒歩2分]
Cafe menu カフェメニュー	soft drinks	各種ソフトドリンク
Animal treats 動物のおやつ	plate of vegetables 200 yen	野菜プレート 200円

Website: http://candyfruit-usagi.net/   Phone: 03-6206-4885

And a few more animals....

Machida Squirrel Garden

Machida

Hundreds of adventurous squirrels live in colorfully decorated houses in Machida Squirrel Garden's spacious outdoor enclosure, sharing their habitat with a couple of friendly giant tortoises. These Taiwan squirrels are very acclimated to human visitors, and will enthusiastically eat out of your hand, or at least out of the protective oven mitt that you'll be issued along with your 100-yen bag of sunflower seeds.

Since you're doling out sunflower seeds one by one—the squirrels have to shell them individually—a single bag will last awhile and is a solid investment. We were taken by surprise when some of the more assertive squirrels jumped onto our arms in order to reach the seeds more easily. Long sleeves are recommended.

Another surprise is that the squirrels here all have names—they're marked on the sides of the houses they live in. (We'll admit, though, that we had trouble telling them apart.)

In front of the squirrel zone is a guinea pig village housing at least a hundred guinea pigs, and some fenced-in pens inhabited by rabbits, small tortoises, chipmunks and prairie dogs. A good-sized plate of lettuce and carrots to feed the hungry critters will set you back another 100 yen, and also lasts a fairly long time.

町田リス園

町田市

　〈町田リス園〉の広々としたフェンスで囲まれた放し飼い広場の色鮮やかな木の巣箱のなかには、何百もの元気のよいリスたちが住んでいる。ここのタイワンリスたちは人によく慣れていて、人間の手から食べ物をもらおうとする。100円でひまわりの種を買って、保護用のミトンをつければエサを与えることができる。
　ひまわりの種は一粒ずつ与えるし、リスたちが皮をむくのに時間がかかる。一袋でしばらくの間楽しめるので、お買い得だ。積極的なリスが種を早く食べたいばかりに、腕に飛び乗ってきたのにはびっくりした。長袖の着用がおすすめだ。
　どうやらここのリスたちは一匹ずつ名前がついているらしいということにも驚いた。木の巣箱の表面に名前が書いてあるのだ。(それでも、誰が誰だか分からない)
　リスの放し飼い広場の向かいはモルモットスペースになっていて、モルモットが少なくとも100匹はいた。他に、うさぎ、リクガメ、シマリス、プレーリードッグがおりで囲まれた飼育場にいた。お腹をすかせた動物たちに与えるレタスやニンジンは100円で買えるが、一皿にたくさんのっているので、かなり長い時間楽しめるだろう。

Overall: ☕☕☕☕☕
総合評価

Visitor amenities: ☕☕☕
店内設備

Animal interactivity: ☕☕☕☕☕
動物とのふれあい

 Data Box

Resident animals 店内にいる動物	squirrels, tortoises, chipmunks, rabbits, prairie dogs and guinea pigs	園内にいる動物　リス、カメ、シマリス、うさぎ、プレーリードッグ、モルモット
Station 最寄駅	Machida	町田
Cover charge 基本料金	400 yen	400 円
Open hours 営業時間	10am-4pm. Closed Tuesdays	10:00 〜 16:00　火曜休園
Address 住所	Machida-shi, Kanaimachi 733-1 [13 minutes by bus from Tsurukawa station (Odakyu line); 14 minutes by bus from Machida station (JR Yokohama line, Odakyu line)]	町田市金内町 733-1 [鶴川駅(小田急線)からバスで13分、町田駅(JR 横浜線、小田急線)からバスで14分]
Cafe menu カフェメニュー	soft drinks and ice cream from vending machines	自動販売機でソフトドリンクとアイスクリームが買える
Animal treats 動物のおやつ	vegetable plate 100 yen, bag of sunflower seeds 100 yen	野菜一皿 100 円　ひまわりの種一袋 100 円

http://www.machida-risuen.com   Phone: 042-734-1001

~ MEMO ~

～ MEMO ～

Animal Cafés
動物カフェ

2015 年 11 月 8 日　第 1 刷発行

著　者　ロブ・サターホワイト＆リチャード・ジェフリー
訳　者　竹内とし江
発行者　浦　晋亮
発行所　IBC パブリッシング株式会社
　　　　〒162-0804 東京都新宿区中里町 29 番 3 号　菱秀神楽坂ビル 9F
　　　　Tel. 03-3513-4511 Fax. 03-3513-4512
　　　　www.ibcpub.co.jp
印刷所　株式会社 メイク

©Robb Satterwhite and Richard Jeffery 2015
©IBC Publishing, Inc. 2015
Printed in Japan

落丁本・乱丁本は、小社宛にお送りください。送料小社負担にてお取り替えいたします。
本書の無断複写(コピー)は著作権法上での例外を除き禁じられています。

ISBN978-4-7946-0377-7